D

MW00982334

Amazing
HOCKEY
TRIVIA

GREYSTONE BOOKS
Douglas & McIntyre Publishing Group
Vancouver/Toronto/New York

For Dick Irvin: too young to retire a hockey legend

Greystone Books
A division of Douglas & McIntyre Ltd.
2323 Quebec Street, Suite 201
Vancouver, British Columbia
Canada V5T 4S7
www.greystonebooks.com

NATIONAL LIBRARY OF CANADA CATALOGUING IN PUBLICATION DATA
Weekes, Don
    Amazing hockey trivia

    ISBN 1-55054-941-3

    1. National Hockey League—Miscellanea. 2. Hockey—Miscellanea. I. Banks, Kerry, 1952– II. Title.
GV847.W348 2002   796.962'64   C2002-910697-4

Editing by Christine Kondo
Cover Design by Peter Cocking
Cover photograph by Bruce Bennett/Bruce Bennett Studios
Typeset by Tanya Lloyd Kyi
Printed and bound in Canada by Friesens
Printed on acid-free paper ∞

We gratefully acknowledge the financial support of the Canada Council for the Arts, the British Columbia Ministry of Tourism, Small Business and Culture, and the Government of Canada through the Book Publishing Industry Development Program (BPIDP) for our publishing activities.

Don Weekes *is a television producer-director at* CTV *in Montreal. This is his nineteenth hockey trivia book.*

Kerry Banks *is an award-winning magazine journalist and sports columnist with Vancouver's* Georgia Straight. *He is the author of ten books including* Pavel Bure: The Riddle of the Russian Rocket *and four titles in the* Hockey Heroes *series.*

CONTENTS

Preface   v

1   THE HOME OPENER   1

Answers   6

Game 1: Hockey Crossword   16

2   THUNDER STICKS   18

Answers   21

Game 2: Frère Jacques (French 101)   29

3   FIRST LIGHT   30

Answers   33

Game 3: The First Five-Team 20-Goal Man   40

4   DYNASTY ROW   42

Answers   46

Game 4: *Not*-Wayne-Gretzky-Offensive Records   54

5   MASKED MARVELS   55

Answers   58

Game 5: Bloodlines   66

6   GRETZKY GOLD   68

Answers   73

Game 6: Olympic Mettle   82

7   TRUE OR FALSE?   83

Answers   86

Game 7: Odd Man Out   94

8   BAD TO THE BONE   95

Answers   98

Game 8: MVP Maverick   105

9   STANLEY IS IN THE BUILDING   106

Answers   111

Solutions to Games   119

Acknowledgements   122

PREFACE

The full-page ad in *Goalies' World* magazine left nothing and everything to the imagination. A prominent NHL goaltender, Carolina's Arturs Irbe, was seeking a Jofa 724 cage and a 281 or 282 helmet. Such a circumstance—asking the public's assistance for a piece of equipment so invaluable to one's livelihood—might just be unprecedented. It also sounds a little desperate. Although Irbe's favourite type of headgear, an old-style wire cage and bubble helmet, was discontinued by its Swedish manufacturer 10 or 15 years ago, the classified ad demonstrates the eccentric nature of those rare individuals who qualify as NHL goaltenders.

As most hockey fans know, Irbe is no more or no less weird than his brethren between the pipes. But he is resolutely old-fashioned. He still repairs his own padding, much of it the same type he wore playing in his native Latvia in the 1980s. His sewing kit, with needles, thread, glue and extra foam padding, is ever-present, and he's been seen patching a torn leg pad between periods of a game. As a traditionalist, Irbe follows in the skate strides of hockey's most famous innovators. For example, Boston great Frank Brimsek built bamboo ribbing into his stick glove and invented the first blocker. Emile Francis of Chicago designed the first goalie trapper by sewing a hockey glove gauntlet cuff onto a first baseman's mitt.

Goalies, however eccentric, and their equipment have revolutionized the style of puck-stopping. (And we're not talking about Patrick Roy's ritual of wrapping the knob of his stick with exactly 60 revolutions of tape, one for each minute of a game.) With better and lighter equipment, today's goaltenders react faster (which has brought about the lowest goals-per-game averages in decades). Their techniques have evolved from the stand-up to the crouch to the butterfly stance. They can now block the lower two-thirds of the net by going down and splaying their legs at the knees.

Even that style is changing. Roy, who spawned a generation of butterfly netminders, is standing up a little more, catching and deflecting shots in an upright position. Martin Brodeur, a stand-up goalie, butter-flies in scrambles. Winning netminders practise a marriage of stand-up and butterfly. It's a matter of evolution, just like their equipment.

"I remember making my first goalie glove from scratch," said Irbe. "I was 10 and I took my dad's leather glove and added some scrap that I found around the house, old clothes and stuff, and I made that glove. I had a hockey book and I patterned my glove after that. I loved doing it and I've never stopped since."

In this our nineteenth hockey trivia book, we look at the eccentrics, innovators and other amazing personalities who have taken our game from thin layers of cotton, felt and leather to state-of-the-art armour.

Get ready for a barrage of shots on every aspect of hockey trivia. Like today's best netminders, expect a few bumps and bruises to reach the win column.

DON WEEKES & KERRY BANKS
March 2002

1
THE HOME OPENER

For 75 consecutive years, each Toronto Maple Leafs' home opener featured an appearance by the 48th Highlanders Scottish marching band, which would stride down the ice with bagpipes blazing. When the team left Maple Leaf Gardens in 1999 and moved to the Air Canada Centre, the 48th regiment was on hand to provide its stirring musical accompaniment. The pipes are calling. Let's drop the puck on our opening chapter of general trivia.

(Answers are on page 6)

1.1 Who is Stanislav Gvoth?
- A. The artist who designed Curtis Joseph's goalie mask
- B. The inventor of the Zamboni
- C. The president of the International Ice Hockey Federation
- D. The Chicago Blackhawks' all-time scoring leader

1.2 Who earned the most first team All-Star selections during his career?
- A. Bobby Hull
- B. Gordie Howe
- C. Wayne Gretzky
- D. Ray Bourque

1.3 How much money did the Colorado Avalanche spend to re-sign Joe Sakic, Patrick Roy and Rob Blake to long-term contracts on June 30, 2001?
- A. US$85 million
- B. US$100 million
- C. US$115 million
- D. US$130 million

1.4 After Pavel Bure was traded to the New York Rangers in March 2002, he switched to No. 9 in honour of what former player?
A. Gordie Howe
B. Maurice Richard
C. Andy Bathgate
D. Valery Kharmalov

1.5 Which goalie wears a mask adorned with the image of Eddie, the menacing mascot of the heavy metal band Iron Maiden?
A. Roman Turek of the Calgary Flames
B. Martin Biron of the Buffalo Sabres
C. Mike Dunham of the Nashville Predators
D. Nikolai Khabibulin of the Tampa Bay Lightning

1.6 On January 27, 2002, the Montreal Canadiens scored their 10,000th goal on home ice. Who notched the milestone goal?
A. Mike Ribeiro
B. Patrick Traverse
C. Benoit Brunet
D. Sergei Berezin

1.7 Which team iced the FLY Line in 2001–02?
A. The Washington Capitals
B. The New York Rangers
C. The Vancouver Canucks
D. The St. Louis Blues

1.8 Which Hall of Famer auctioned off most of his personal hockey memorabilia in 2001, raising US$400,000 in the process?
A. Glenn Hall
B. Mike Bossy
C. Guy Lafleur
D. Frank Mahovlich

1.9 How many goals did Brett Hull score against Dallas the first time he returned to Texas to play his former team as a member of the Detroit Red Wings on October 31, 2001?
   A. One goal
   B. Two goals
   C. Three goals
   D. Brett Hull didn't score

1.10 Which Canadian rock band was featured on the NHL's official 2002 video game?
   A. Blue Rodeo
   B. Nickelback
   C. The Tragically Hip
   D. The Barenaked Ladies

1.11 The New York Islanders wore whose name and number on their sweaters during the pre-game warm up on October 20, 2001?
   A. Clark Gilles's No. 9
   B. Bryan Trottier's No. 19
   C. Mike Bossy's No. 22
   D. Bob Nystrom's No. 23

1.12 What important Toronto Maple Leafs historical artefact did former Leafs broadcaster Brian McFarlane save from destruction in 1970?
   A. The Leafs' Stanley Cup banners
   B. Archival film footage of Leafs' games
   C. Foster Hewitt's broadcasting gondola
   D. The Leafs' original team charter

1.13 In 2000, CCM was asked to design a special type of skate for what kind of animal?
   A. A dog
   B. A bear
   C. A chimpanzee
   D. A kangaroo

1.14 In 2000–01, which team became the first to use a video device called XOS Sketch, as a strategic tool on the bench during games?
   A. The Atlanta Thrashers
   B. The Washington Capitals
   C. The Vancouver Canucks
   D. The Los Angeles Kings

1.15 What is the record for most goals in a season by a player who did not score a single power-play goal?
   A. 21 goals
   B. 26 goals
   C. 31 goals
   D. 36 goals

1.16 What is the largest crowd to ever attend a hockey game?
   A. 28,554 fans
   B. 42,554 fans
   C. 58,554 fans
   D. 74,554 fans

1.17 Which player lost the most teeth in 2001–02?
   A. Mike Ricci of the San Jose Sharks
   B. Doug Weight of the St. Louis Blues
   C. Ilya Kovalchuk of the Atlanta Thrashers
   D. Martin Straka of the Pittsburgh Penguins

1.18 Most players record more assists than goals, but for some snipers the reverse is true. Who holds the NHL mark for the largest goals-to-assists differential in a season?

A. Brett Hull
B. Pavel Bure
C. Cam Neely
D. Lanny McDonald

1.19 How many more games did Detroit great Ted Lindsay need to play to become the NHL's first 1,000-game man when he retired after the 1959–60 season?

A. One game
B. 10 games
C. 20 games
D. 70 games

1.20 Which former Montreal Canadiens player had a lake named after him in 2001?

A. Guy Lafleur
B. Doug Harvey
C. Jean Béliveau
D. Maurice Richard

1.21 According to the Hockey Hall of Fame, the world's oldest hockey stick was carved in what year?

A. 1752
B. 1802
C. 1852
D. 1902

1.22 What is greatest number of games a team has finished above
.500 during the regular season and still not made the playoffs?
A. Four games
B. Eight games
C. 12 games
D. 16 games

1.23 Which goalie established his own charitable foundation to
fund a hockey program for underprivileged youth in 2001?
A. Dominik Hasek
B. Mike Richter
C. Patrick Roy
D. Martin Brodeur

THE HOME OPENER
Answers

1.1 **D. The Chicago Blackhawks' all-time scoring leader**
Stanislav Gvoth was born on May 20, 1940, in Sokolce, Czechoslovakia. When the Communists seized control of the country in
1948, Mr. and Mrs. Gvoth made a difficult decision and decided
to send their son to Canada to live with his Uncle Joe and Aunt
Anna in St. Catharines, Ontario. Little Stan took their last name,
Mikita, as his own. He would later make it one of the most
famous names in NHL annals. The 1,467 career points that
Mikita compiled during his 22-year career are the most by a
player in a Blackhawks uniform.

1.2 **D. Ray Bourque**
No less an authority than three-time Norris Trophy winner Chris
Chelios has said: "Ray Bourque is the best defenseman I have
seen." Many would agree. Bourque is certainly the best rearguard
of his era. No specialist, he excelled at all aspects of the game:

skating, hitting, scoring, passing and defensive-zone coverage. To understand how dominant a force Bourque was, you only need to scan his 13 first All-Star team selections, the most of any player in NHL history. His total is one more than Gordie Howe's, three more than Bobby Hull's and five more than Wayne Gretzky's. Bourque earned his 13th selection to the first All-Star team in 2000–01, at age 40.

1.3   C. US$115 million
In a wild spending spree just after the 2001 NHL Entry Draft, the Stanley Cup champion Colorado Avalanche doled out an unprecedented US$115 million to re-sign three of its big stars: centre Joe Sakic, goalie Patrick Roy and defenseman Rob Blake. Altogether, Sakic (US$9.8 million), Roy (US$8.5 million) and Blake (US$9.3 million) earned almost US$28 million in 2001–02, more than the entire rosters of seven NHL teams.

1.4   B. Maurice Richard
When big stars are traded they often make a point of asking for the same number they wore before. But Pavel Bure broke with tradition after the Florida Panthers traded him to the New York Rangers on March 19, 2002. Instead of his customary No. 10, which was being worn by Rangers winger Sandy McCarthy, Bure asked for No. 9. The move was meant to honour his namesake, Maurice "Rocket" Richard, who made the number famous with the Montreal Canadiens. As the Russian Rocket explained: "Rocket Richard wore No. 9 and it was available. I won his trophy (the Richard Trophy for top goal-scorer in the league) twice. I think it's a good number." Prior to claiming the number, Bure placed a call to fan favourite Adam Graves, who wore No. 9 in Manhattan for a decade before being traded to the San Jose Sharks in the summer of 2001. Graves assured Bure there was no problem.

1.5 A. Roman Turek of the Calgary Flames
The Czech goalie has been a serious fan of Iron Maiden since he was a teenager. In fact, he counts a backstage meeting with the heavy metal band at a concert in Germany as one of his top thrills. At the time, Turek was playing with Nurnberg of the German Elite League. As he admitted in an interview with the *Calgary Sun:* "After the concert, one guy took me to their locker room and they gave me CDs, a T-shirt and a hat. I already played with the group's mascot Eddie painted on my mask, they signed it and I just said, 'Oh, my God! That's my dream come true.'" Eddie is also Turek's nickname and the name of his nine-year-old son.

1.6 D. Sergei Berezin
Sergei Berezin won't likely forget his first goal for the Montreal Canadiens: it was the 10,000th home-ice goal scored by a Canadiens player. Montreal became the first NHL team to reach the milestone in its 2,675th regular-season home game. Berezin, the 703rd player to pull on a Habs jersey, was playing just his second game with Montreal after being acquired in a trade with the Phoenix Coyotes. He only became aware of his achievement when team officials asked him to give up his stick as a piece of memorabilia. "I don't think it's fair for me to get it because a lot of Montreal Canadiens scored a lot of goals over so many years, and I just got here last night, but I'll take it," said Berezin. The historic goal, which proved to be the game-winner in a 3–1 victory over the San Jose Sharks, was assisted by Doug Gilmour and Yanic Perreault. Like Berezin, both were playing their first season for Montreal, and also like Berezin, both were former Maple Leafs. Another oddity: it's believed to be the first time in NHL history that all three players who picked up points on a goal wore numbers in the nineties: 93 (Gilmour), 94 (Perreault) and 95 (Berezin).

1.7 B. The New York Rangers
Until Eric Lindros ran into injury problems midway through 2001–02, he and his two wingers, Theo Fleury and Mike York, formed the league's highest-scoring trio. The FLY Line, as the New York media dubbed it, was an unconventional unit, with the hulking Lindros flanked by two speedy, but undersized wingers. Joked Fleury: "I don't understand all this talk about Lindros needing a big winger. If you put me and Yorkie together, we're 11-foot one."

1.8 C. Guy Lafleur
Stanley Cup rings, trophies, jerseys, pucks, sticks and skates amassed over Guy Lafleur's illustrious 17-year career were available at the auction which lasted two weeks and was conducted via the Internet and by telephone. The most expensive of the 122 items was Lafleur's 1977 Conn Smythe Trophy, which sold for US$24,423. His 1977 Hart Trophy fetched US$21,839, while four of the Hall of Famer's Cup rings went for between US$10,000 and US$15,000 each. Even Lafleur's frayed first pair of skates, which he wore as a five-year-old, found a buyer for US$4,512. Lafleur, who claimed he had no personal attachment to the items, said he would donate US$25,000 to charity and keep the rest of the proceeds.

1.9 B. Two goals
Demonstrating a flair for the dramatic, Brett Hull set up one goal and scored twice in his first game against his former team, including the game-winner, which he wired past goalie Ed Belfour 52 seconds into overtime. For Hull, who signed with Detroit in the off-season after Dallas declined to offer him a contract, the result was sweet. Asked by reporters if he would be content to play second fiddle on the Red Wings' star-packed team, Hull replied: "I'll play the tuba. I don't care as long as we keep winning and having fun."

1.10   D. The Barenaked Ladies
It might just be the all-time best Canadian music gig. Not only did the Toronto band contribute three songs to the NHL 2002 video-game soundtrack, the game's designers even included the band members in the game along with the other NHL players. "Seeing myself as a member of the Toronto Maple Leafs is a boyhood fantasy," said Ladies drummer Tyler Stewart. "For me it was very exciting to know that I could make it to the NHL—even if it is only on a digital level."

1.11   B. Bryan Trottier's No. 19
On October 20, 2001, Trottier became the sixth Islander to have his number retired, joining previous honourees Denis Potvin, Mike Bossy, Clark Gillies, Bob Nystrom and Billy Smith. Although long overdue, the occasion was handled with class. Trottier amassed a franchise-high 1,353 points in 15 seasons with the Islanders and won four Stanley Cups. He would add two more Cups with the Pittsburgh Penguins in 1991 and 1992. Few teams could contain the hard-driving centre during his prime, and the sight of all the Islanders players circling the ice with Trottier's name and number made a vivid impression on visiting San Jose Sharks coach Darryl Sutter. "I told Trots that if 20 years ago, I'd seen 20 Bryan Trottiers skating around before a game, I would've just lay down at centre ice."

1.12   B. Archival film footage of Leafs' games
In 1970, Harold Ballard, then part-owner of the Toronto Maple Leafs, ordered a storage room at Maple Leaf Gardens cleaned out and hundreds of canisters of film tossed in the garbage. Brian McFarlane, a Leafs broadcaster and hockey historian, learned about the stockpile just before it was about to be destroyed. He rescued a total of 796 cans and stored them at his own expense at a film distribution outlet in Toronto. The cache included all of the Leafs' game footage from 1962 to 1969, the era in which the club won four Stanley Cups. The film remained in storage until

2001, when the club prepared to launch Leafs TV. McFarlane then sold the film to Molson Inc., Leafs TV's major sponsor. It was still in pristine condition and is now considered to be Leafs TV's most valuable asset.

1.13 **C. A chimpanzee**

Andre Joly, manager of CCM's skate factory in St. Jean, Quebec, was more than a little sceptical when he received a phone call asking if the company could design a pair of hockey skates for a chimpanzee. "At first I thought it was a joke, and even after I received the chimp's foot tracing, I still thought it was a joke," admitted Joly. But the caller, film director Robert Vince, was serious. Vince needed them for Jack, the simian star of a new film he was making, *MVP: Most Valuable Primate*. "The skates we ended up designing basically combined a size-three junior skate with a size-eight toe cap," said Joly. Incredibly, it only took Jack about eight weeks to learn to skate, use a hockey stick and shoot a puck. If hockey and chimpanzees sound like an unlikely combo, Vince says that's simply because you don't know chimps. "They like anything that involves speed and aggression and feeling the wind blowing in their face."

1.14 **B. The Washington Capitals**

The Capitals' coaching staff began using the XOS Sketch on the bench at the start of the 2000–01 season. The US$50,000 video system, which is operated by using a stylus on a touch screen, is primarily a teaching tool. Among those impressed with the system's quick feedback was Capitals winger Peter Bondra, who credited the device with helping him improve his performance on the power play. "You don't have to wait until the period is over," noted Bondra. "Right after a shift you can see what type of box opponents have and then adjust." After the introduction of the XOS Sketch, the Capitals' power play rose from 21st overall in 1999–2000 to fourth best in the league in 2000–01.

1.15   C. 31 goals

Reaching more than 30 goals in a season without counting a single goal on the power play is a rare achievement. In fact, it's happened only once in NHL history. The marksman was Winnipeg Jets left-winger Doug Smail, who tallied 31 goals in 1984–85. The 31 goals was a single-season high for the Moose Jaw-native, who was usually employed in a checking role by the Jets. In fact, of the 210 goals Smail scored in his career, only eight came on the power play.

MOST GOALS IN A SEASON WITHOUT SCORING A POWER-PLAY GOAL

Player	Team	Season	Goals
Doug Smail	Winnipeg	1984–85	31
John Wensink	Boston	1978–79	28
Stan Jonathan	Boston	1977–78	27
Bob Errey	Pittsburgh	1988–89	26

1.16   D. 74,554 fans

On October 6, 2001, the Michigan State Spartans and Michigan Wolverines university hockey teams played to a 3–3 tie in the 238th meeting of their storied rivalry. But this game was different. It was played outdoors on an artificial ice rink set on a football field at Spartan Stadium in front of 74,554 fans. Gordie Howe dropped the puck for the ceremonial opening face-off and flame-throwers belched fire at each corner of the rink. There was even a laser-light show and prancing cheerleaders. "It was the greatest night ever for college hockey," declared Wolverines coach Red Berenson. "It was a great game in a great setting." The crowd was the largest ever assembled for a hockey game, surpassing the 55,000 who watched Sweden defeat the USSR 3–2 at the 1957 World Championships in Moscow.

1.17 C. Ilya Kovalchuk of the Atlanta Thrashers
The 18-year-old Russian rookie lost nine of his teeth, but it wasn't the result of getting a stick in the face. Kovalchuk had four wisdom teeth extracted and five rotten ones extracted. In Russia, the water is not treated with fluoride, and Kovalchuk clearly didn't heed the advice to brush three times a day, much to the chagrin of his mother, a dental hygienist. Kovalchuk was unconcerned by the loss of his pearlies. "I have no problem," he said, through the aid of an interpreter. "The only difference is I know they are not there."

1.18 A. Brett Hull
In his prime, Brett Hull was a goal-scoring machine. In 1990–91, with the St. Louis Blues, he notched 86 goals to go with 45 assists, by far the largest goals-to-assists differential in NHL history. In fact, the winger owns three of the top five rankings in the category. Hull was aided in 1990–91 by the precision passing of centre Adam Oates, who collected 90 assists, the most ever by a St. Louis player.

LARGEST SINGLE-SEASON GOALS-TO-ASSISTS DIFFERENTIALS

Player	Team	Season	G	A	Dif
Brett Hull	St. Louis	1990–91	86	45	41
Lanny McDonald	Calgary	1982–83	66	32	34
Brett Hull	St. Louis	1989–90	72	41	31
Brett Hull	St. Louis	1991–92	70	39	31
Reggie Leach	Philadelphia	1975–76	61	30	31

1.19 A. One game
When Lindsay retired after the 1959–60 season, he had scored more goals than any other left-winger (365), accumulated more penalty minutes than any other player (1,635) and had played in

more regular-season games than any other player (999). Strangely, he called it quits despite needing only one more game to become the NHL's first 1,000-game man. On November 26, 1961, Howe eclipsed Lindsay's mark and became the first to skate in 1,000 games. In 1964–65, after four years of retirement, Lindsay returned to play one more season with the Detroit Red Wings, adding 69 games to his aggregate. And, just to prove he hadn't gone soft, the 39-year-old warhorse registered 173 penalty minutes, the second-highest total of his career, and only four minutes behind the NHL's penalty-minute leader that year, Carl Brewer.

1.20 D. Maurice Richard
Fishing was one of the Rocket's favourite pastimes, so it's fitting that the Quebec government decided to honour his memory by renaming one of his favourite fishing spots after him. Lac Maurice-Richard, located 180 kilometres north of Montreal, is unlikely to become a shrine for hockey fans because it can only be reached by float plane or a two-day trek through the bush. Richard first began coming to the isolated, horseshoe-shaped lake (formerly known as Lac Bent) in 1966, and he continued to visit it until 1999, a year before his death from stomach cancer.

1.21 C. 1852
The world's oldest existing hockey stick was carved sometime around 1852 from a piece of hickory by Alexander Rutherford Sr. at his farm outside Lindsay, Ontario. The stick was handed down through the family to Gord Sharpe of Peterborough, Ontario. Sharpe, who had the stick's age verified by the Hockey Hall of Fame, decided to put it up for sale on eBay's Web site in 2001. His asking price? A cool $US2 million. That estimate proved a bit too exorbitant. Sharpe didn't get any takers.

1.22 D. 16 games
Finishing 16 games above .500 would easily assure a playoff berth today, but in 1969–70, the defending-champion Montreal

Canadiens went 38–22–16 and still failed to make the post-season. The reason was the NHL's unbalanced divisional playoffs format. Montreal's division, the East, featured strong, established teams, while the West was composed of third-year expansion clubs. Although the teams played an interlocking schedule, only four teams from each division, rather than the top eight overall, made the playoffs. Montreal's 92 points—which would have led the West and was only seven points back of the East division-champion Blackhawks and Bruins—left it tied with the New York Rangers for the fourth and final playoff spot. New York qualified for the postseason because it had scored more goals than Montreal.

1.23 A. Dominik Hasek

Hasek may have left Buffalo for Detroit after the 2000–01 season, but the Czech-born goalie also left an enduring legacy in his adopted city. In March 2001, Hasek donated US$1 million of his own money to establish his own charitable foundation called Hasek's Heroes, which funds a hockey and skating program for underprivileged Buffalo youth. "I realize not every boy or girl is as lucky as my children," said Hasek, a father of two. "I want to create a situation where quality training, quality equipment and experienced coaches will not be an issue. They will be a standard." A total of 187 children, ages six to 14, enrolled in the program's inaugural season.

Game 1

HOCKEY CROSSWORD

(Solutions are on page 119)

Across

1. Detroit's Steve _____
5. Detroit's Brendan _____
10. Calgary/St. Louis's Cory _____
11. NYR's Eric _____
12. Pittsburgh/Colorado's Darius _____
16. Ottawa's Radek _____
19. Toronto's Garry _____
20. Old-timer, retired in 1973, Montreal's Dave _____
21. 17-year veteran Murray _____
24. "_____ and grab" hockey
26. Edmonton _____
27. Colorado's Patrick _____
29. Old-time NYR goalie Chuck _____
30. Eight-year veteran Todd _____
31. Paper or electronic _____
35. One-time Florida goalie John _____
37. Abbreviation for overtime
39. Buffalo tough guy Rob _____
40. Retired Buffalo Sabre Mark _____
41. Ottawa's Wade _____

Down

1. Toronto's Dmitry _____
2. New Jersey's Patrik _____
3. Florida/St. Louis's Scott _____
4. _____ Broten
6. Brett _____
7. Gordie Howe's uniform No. _____
8. From pucks to donuts, Tim _____
9. St. Louis's Tyson _____
13. Anaheim's Antti _____
14. NYI's John _____
15. _____ Apps Jr. and Sr.
17. Anaheim's Paul _____
18. NYR's Theo _____
22. 500-goal man Pat _____
23. 13-year veteran Uwe _____
25. Detroit D-man Chris _____
28. Don Cherry once called Pavel Bure this kind of animal
32. Buffalo's Miroslav _____

33. Old-timer, Toronto's _____ Bathgate

34. Bland colour

36. _____ Krupp

38. Old-timer _____ Van Impe

2
THUNDER STICKS

Bobby Hull's slap shot was a fearsome weapon. One of his screamers was timed at 119.5 MPH. Johnny Bower said that stopping one of the Golden Jet's blasts was "like being slugged by a sledgehammer." Not only did Hull's shot have tremendous velocity, his curved blade often made the puck curve and dip. It's no accident that shortly after Hull joined the NHL, goalies began wearing masks. In this chapter, we put the radar gun on hockey's big shooters.

(Answers are on page 21)

2.1 Who owns the NHL record for the most goals in a calendar month?
- A. Wayne Gretzky
- B. Teemu Selanne
- C. Brett Hull
- D. Mario Lemieux

2.2 Wayne Gretzky registered an NHL-record 92 goals in an 80-game schedule in 1981–82. In how many games did Gretzky fail to score a goal that season?
- A. 10 games
- B. 15 games
- C. 20 games
- D. 25 games

2.3 Who scored the fastest four goals in NHL history?
- A. Peter Bondra
- B. Mario Lemieux
- C. Paul Kariya
- D. Sergei Fedorov

2.4 Who surpassed Mario Lemieux as the NHL's all-time leader in penalty shots in 2001–02?

A. Steve Yzerman
B. Theo Fleury
C. Pavel Bure
D. Mats Sundin

2.5 Which players shared the mark for the longest consecutive game-scoring streak in 2001–02?

A. Joe Sakic and Mike Modano
B. Jarome Iginla and Todd Bertuzzi
C. Joe Thornton and Brendan Shanahan
D. Eric Daze and Alexei Yashin

2.6 Which scoring milestone did Steve Yzerman and Ron Francis both reach in 2001–02?

A. 600 goals
B. 1,200 assists
C. 500 goals and 1,000 assists
D. 30 career hat tricks

2.7 Which NHL gunner was known as the "Riverton Rifle"?

A. Steve Shutt of the Montreal Canadiens
B. Danny Grant of the Minnesota North Stars
C. Reggie Leach of the Philadelphia Flyers
D. Mickey Redmond of the Detroit Red Wings

2.8 Among players who scored 40 goals in a season, who holds the NHL record for scoring the highest percentage of his goals on the power play?

A. Yvan Cournoyer of the Montreal Canadiens
B. Joe Nieuwendyk of the Calgary Flames
C. Luc Robitaille of the Los Angeles Kings
D. Dave Andreychuk of the Buffalo Sabres

2.9 Who holds the mark for scoring the fewest power-play goals during a season in which he notched 50 goals?
A. Reggie Leach of the Philadelphia Flyers
B. Mark Messier of the Edmonton Oilers
C. Joe Mullen of the Calgary Flames
D. Steve Yzerman of the Detroit Red Wings

2.10 In how many consecutive seasons did Gordie Howe finish in the top 10 of the NHL scoring race?
A. 12 seasons
B. 15 seasons
C. 18 seasons
D. 21 seasons

2.11 Who is the youngest player to score five goals in an NHL game?
A. Mats Sundin
B. Wayne Gretzky
C. Don Murdoch
D. Bryan Trottier

2.12 Which company introduced a revolutionary high-tech hockey stick called the Synergy in 2000–01?
A. Koho
B. Easton
C. Bauer
D. Cooper

2.13 Which NHLer would superstitiously break his stick each time he scored a goal?
A. Petr Klima
B. Pierre Larouche
C. Al Iafrate
D. Geoff Courtnall

2.14 Who holds the record for collecting the most points in his final NHL season?
A. Mike Bossy
B. Bobby Clarke
C. Hakan Loob
D. Frank Mahovlich

2.15 What is the NHL record for most goals scored in a season by a player who had no assists?
A. Seven goals
B. 10 goals
C. 13 goals
D. 16 goals

2.16 Which rookie of the year posted the biggest increase in points in his second season?
A. Pavel Bure
B. Mike Bossy
C. Mario Lemieux
D. Peter Stastny

THUNDER STICKS
Answers

2.1 B. Teemu Selanne
Most hockey analysts predicted that Finnish rookie Teemu Selanne would have trouble adjusting to the NHL style of play in his first season. They were wrong. Selanne struck for a hat trick in his fifth game with the Winnipeg Jets in 1992–93, and never looked back. On March 2, 1993, Selanne scored his 54th goal of the season, breaking Mike Bossy's NHL record for most goals by a rookie. He celebrated by tossing one glove up in the air, then

dropped to one knee and pointed his stick like a rifle as he pretended to shoot it out of the air. The Finnish Flash went on a wild tear in March, firing 20 goals, the most ever by an NHLer in one calendar month. Selanne ended the season with 76 goals, obliterating Bossy's rookie mark.

2.2 D. 25 games
Although shell-shocked opposition goalies might dispute it, Wayne Gretzky wasn't unstoppable in 1981–82. There were 25 games in which he failed to light the lamp. Gretzky's race to 92 goals was powered by a series of offensive explosions. The Edmonton Oilers' dynamo had six three-goal games, three four-goal games and one five-goal game that year. In other words, he scored nearly 40 per cent of his goals in just 10 games. Gretzky didn't give anyone a break though, scoring against every team in the league while racking up his best total against Los Angeles: 13 goals. If you subtract the 25 contests in which Gretzky didn't score in 1981–82, you're left with this startling stat: he amassed his 92 goals in 55 games.

2.3 A. Peter Bondra
Bondra was in a gunner's groove on February 5, 1994. The Washington Capitals winger lit up Tampa Bay Lightning goalie Daren Puppa like a cheap cigar, snapping home four goals in a span of four minutes and 12 seconds in the first period. It was the fastest four-goal outburst in NHL history. To top things off, Bondra added a fifth marker in the Caps' 6–3 victory.

2.4 C. Pavel Bure
Who else, but the Breakaway Kid? The speedy Russian was awarded the eighth and ninth penalty shots of his career in 2001–02 with the Florida Panthers, surpassing Mario Lemieux as the NHL's all-time leader in the category. In a bizarre twist, not only did Bure not score on either attempt, he didn't even register a shot on net. In the first case, on January 25, 2002, Bure lost con-

trol of the puck on a bad patch of ice while skating in on Carolina Hurricanes netminder Arturs Irbe, then tripped while trying to dig it out of his skates and slid into the end boards. On his record-setting ninth penalty shot, taken against Boston Bruins goalie Byron Dafoe on February 9, 2002, the Russian Rocket lost the handle while trying a backhand deke and wound up ringing the puck off the outside of the post. A frustrated Bure said after the game: "That's the way it is. If I scored on every breakaway I had this year I'd have 90 goals." All told, Bure has scored on five of his nine attempts, while Lemieux has been successful on six of his eight.

2.5 **B. Jarome Iginla and Todd Bertuzzi**
Jarome Iginla and Todd Bertuzzi both enjoyed breakout seasons in 2001–02, posting league-high 15 consecutive-game points streaks. Iginla collected 18 goals and 13 assists in 15 straight games for the Calgary Flames from October 18 to November 22, an offensive surge that helped him win a spot on Canada's Olympic squad. Bertuzzi counted six goals and 12 assists in a 15-game scoring streak from January 3 to January 28, helping to lift the Vancouver Canucks into playoff contention.

2.6 **C. 500 goals and 1,000 assists**
Membership in the elite 500-goal, 1,000-assist club grew from four to six players in 2001–02, as Ron Francis and Steve Yzerman joined members Wayne Gretzky, Gordie Howe, Mark Messier and Marcel Dionne. Francis became the fifth NHLer to reach the milestone, when the Carolina captain scored his 500th goal in a 6–3 loss to Boston on January 2, 2002. Yzerman joined the club on January 20, 2002, with his 1,000th assist on Mathieu Dandenault's overtime winner in Detroit's 3–2 victory over Ottawa.

2.7 **C. Reggie Leach of the Philadelphia Flyers**
A natural scorer with the power to connect from the blueline and the finesse to take a pass and wrist a shot in one motion, Leach

had a brief reign in the mid-1970s as one of the NHL's most dangerous snipers. In 1975–76, he topped the league with 61 goals for Philadelphia. Born in Riverton, Manitoba, Leach always took great pride in his shooting ability. He would take hundreds of shots every day at practice, moving the puck around and focussing on specific targets. Unfortunately, he put less effort into other aspects of his game, which along with a weakness for alcohol, contributed to his rather modest career total of 381 goals. With his talent, Leach could have easily scored 500.

2.8   D. Dave Andreychuk of the Buffalo Sabres
Dave Andreychuk may have been the premier power-play specialist in NHL history: more than half of his career goals were scored when his team had the man-advantage. Many came via deflections or rebounds which he banged in from the edge of the crease. At six-foot-four and 220 pounds, Andreychuk was a hard man to move once he had parked himself near the goalie. With the Sabres in 1991–92, the big winger scored 28 of his 41 goals (68 per cent) on the power play. That's the highest percentage ever by a 40-goal scorer.

HIGHEST PERCENTAGE OF GOALS ON THE POWER PLAY
(BY PLAYERS WITH 40-GOAL SEASONS OR MORE)*

Player	Team	Season	G	PPG	Pct
Dave Andreychuk	Buffalo	1991–92	41	28	.68
Joe Nieuwendyk	Calgary	1992–93	51	31	.61
Dave Andreychuk	Buf/Tor	1992–93	54	32	.59
Luc Robitaille	Los Angeles	1991–92	44	26	.59
Tim Kerr	Philadelphia	1985–86	58	34	.59

* since 1967–68

2.9   A. **Reggie Leach of the Philadelphia Flyers**
Because he had such a wicked slap shot, Leach often played the
point on the Flyers' power play, which may partly explain why he
scored only five of his 50 goals in 1979–80 on the power play.
Even so, it's a real eye-opener to see his name at the top of this list.
Obviously, Leach was a major threat to score at even strength, a
common trait among superior players. It's also a surprise to see
Mike Bossy and Jari Kurri so high in the category. They both rou-
tinely posted double-digit goal totals on the power play.

FEWEST POWER-PLAY GOALS BY A 50-GOAL SCORER*

Player	Team	Season	G	PPG
Reggie Leach	Philadelphia	1979–80	50	5
Mike Bossy	NY Islanders	1983–84	51	6
Jari Kurri	Edmonton	1986–87	54	7
Rick Martin	Buffalo	1973–74	52	8
Bobby Hull	Chicago	1971–72	50	8
Danny Gare	Buffalo	1975–76	50	8
Steve Shutt	Montreal	1976–77	60	8
Wayne Gretzky	Edmonton	1984–85	73	8

* since 1967–68

2.10   D. **21 seasons**
Take a long look at that number. Incredible isn't it? For 21
straight seasons, Gordie Howe ranked among the NHL's top 10
scorers. Not only did Howe never have a bad year, he seemed
impervious to injury: he didn't miss more than six games in any
season during those 21 years. The string began in 1949–50,
Howe's fourth year in the league, and continued until 1969–70.
Mr. Hockey led the loop in scoring six times, had one second-
place finish and six thirds.

2.11 C. Don Murdoch

The New York Rangers figured they had a budding superstar in Murdoch, especially after the rookie winger blitzed Minnesota North Stars goalie Gary Smith for five goals in a 10–4 rout on October 12, 1976. Murdoch was two weeks shy of turning 20 and in just his fourth NHL game. A mid-season ankle injury cost him the rookie-of-the-year award, but he still finished with 32 goals and 56 points in 59 games. But after a sophomore season of 55 points in 66 games, Murdoch ran into trouble with the law. In the summer of 1978, a routine search by customs officers in Toronto led to the discovery of 4.8 grams of cocaine stashed in one of his socks and five marijuana joints inside a cigarette packet. Although Murdoch didn't get any jail time for the drug charge, he was suspended for the first 40 games of the 1978–79 season. Having all that idle time didn't help the youngster, who had a fondness for Manhattan's nightlife. When he returned to action, he had lost some of his spark. By 1982, Murdoch was playing in the minors and never made it back to the NHL.

2.12 B. Easton

Midway through the 2001–02 season about 180 NHLers were using the Easton Synergy, a one-piece stick made of a mixture of carbon-graphite and Kevlar. At 460 grams, it's one-third lighter than most wooden models, yet is still strong and flexible. The Synergy can supposedly increase the velocity of an NHLer's shot by as much as 10 per cent, and because the manufacturing process produces a consistent curve, players no longer have to spend hours fine-tuning their blades. Other companies have rushed to join the composite revolution, leading some to suggest that this new breed of stick could swing the balance back in favour of shooters after a long period of dominance by goalies. The masked men are worried. As Detroit Red Wings netminder Manny Legace noted, "A guy like Al MacInnis could be up there around a buck twenty [120 MPH] if he starts using these new sticks. That's getting scary."

2.13 **A. Petr Klima**
Some players name their sticks, some kiss them for luck, others give them pep talks, but Klima's superstition was unique. The eccentric Czech forward would use a stick only until he scored with it. Then he'd deliberately break the lumber, believing that each stick only had one goal in it. Considering that he recorded 408 regular-season and playoff goals in his career, Klima must have been an equipment manager's worst nightmare.

2.14 **C. Hakan Loob**
No player ever departed the NHL on a higher note than Hakan Loob. In his last season in 1988–89, the 28-year-old winger amassed 85 points on 27 goals and 58 assists for the Calgary Flames and helped his club win the Stanley Cup. After the season, Loob returned home to Sweden, where he skated for seven more years in the Swedish Elite League and played for his country in two Olympics and two World Championships.

MOST POINTS IN FINAL NHL SEASON					
Player	**Team**	**Season**	**G**	**A**	**P**
Hakan Loob	Calgary	1988–89	27	58	85
Frank Mahovlich	Montreal	1973–74	31	49	80
Jean Béliveau	Montreal	1970–71	25	51	76
Mike Bossy	NY Islanders	1986–87	38	37	75
Johnny McKenzie	Boston	1971–72	22	47	69

2.15 **C. 13 goals**
It took a lot of digging to discover the owner of this oddball record. His name? John McKinnon of the Pittsburgh Pirates in 1926–27. Amazingly, McKinnon was a defenseman. Although NHL scorekeepers awarded fewer assists in the 1920s than they do today, it's still hard to imagine how a defenseman could register 13 goals without picking up a single assist. Judging by his career numbers—28 goals, 11 assists—McKinnon definitely preferred

shooting to passing. The closest challenger to McKinnon that we could find was Mickey Roach, who scored 11 goals without an assist for the New York Americans in 1926–27.

2.16 A. Pavel Bure
The sophomore jinx is no myth. Many star rookies have trouble improving in their second year, partly because other teams are more aware of them, but also because the expectations placed on them are so much greater. Calder Trophy winners who defy the odds and improve in year two are rare commodities. The largest leap in points by a Calder winner belongs to Pavel Bure. After posting 60 points with the Vancouver Canucks in 1991–92, he upped his output to 110 in his sophomore year, a jump of 50 points. The Russian Rocket's goal count alone zoomed from 34 to 60. Bure's totals in his rookie campaign would have undoubtedly been higher had he played a full season, but a contract wrangle with Russian hockey officials delayed his debut with the Canucks until November 1991.

BIGGEST IMPROVEMENTS IN POINTS
BY CALDER TROPHY WINNERS*

Player	Team	Seasons	Points	Increase
Pavel Bure	Vancouver	1991–92	60	
		1992–93	110	50
Mario Lemieux	Pittsburgh	1984–85	100	
		1985–86	141	41
Mike Bossy	NY Islanders	1977–78	91	
		1978–79	126	35
Peter Stastny	Quebec	1980–81	109	
		1981–82	139	30
Luc Robitaille	Los Angeles	1986–87	84	
		1987–88	111	27

*Peter Forsberg's 66-point leap in points in his second year is discounted because his rookie season was the lockout-shortened 1994–95 campaign.

Game 2
FRÈRE JACQUES
(FRENCH 101)

In 1909, Ottawa businessman J. Ambrose O'Brien founded an "all French-Canadian team" he called "le Canadien," a nickname originally given to French explorers and settlers of Canada during the 1700s. The Montreal Canadiens became hockey's greatest dynasty and French-speaking players proved to be among the most elite puck shooters and stoppers. Listed below are 12 NHLers with French names (including a few born outside of Quebec). Match the player's *nom de famille* and its literal English translation.

(*Solutions are on page 119*)

1. _____	Patrick Roy	A.	The Flower
2. _____	Pat LaFontaine	B.	Small
3. _____	Simon Gagné	C.	The Rider
4. _____	Eric Desjardins	D.	The Major
5. _____	Michel Petit	E.	King
6. _____	Guy Lafleur	F.	The Best
7. _____	Jacques Lemaire	G.	The Gardens
8. _____	Vincent Lecavalier	H.	Side
9. _____	Wilf Paiement	I.	Little Bit of Love
10. _____	Sylvain Côté	J.	The Fountain
11. _____	Rod Brind'Amour	K.	Payment
12. _____	Mario Lemieux	L.	Win

3

FIRST LIGHT

Maurice Richard scored many historic goals, but one that is rarely mentioned was a power-play marker on October 9, 1956, at the All-Star game. After Richard scored, Red Sullivan of the All-Stars left the penalty box and skated back on the ice. This was an NHL first. Up until the 1956–57 season, players always had to serve the full duration of their penalties, whether a team scored with the man-advantage or not.

(Answers are on page 33)

3.1 Who was the first NHLer to record 100 points in six consecutive seasons?
A. Phil Esposito
B. Bobby Orr
C. Guy Lafleur
D. Wayne Gretzky

3.2 The first NHLer born outside of Canada to score 50 goals in a season came from which country?
A. Finland
B. Sweden
C. England
D. USA

3.3 In which city did the first North American telecast of an NHL game take place?
A. Toronto
B. Montreal
C. New York
D. Chicago

3.4 Who is the first NHLer to win both the hardest-shot and the fastest-skater categories at the All-Star skills competition?

A. Sergei Fedorov
B. Pavel Bure
C. Peter Bondra
D. Bill Guerin

3.5 What is the oldest age at which a goalie made his first appearance in the NHL playoffs?

A. 37
B. 39
C. 41
D. 43

3.6 Which was the first line to feature three 100-point scorers?

A. New York's GAG Line (Ratelle, Gilbert, Hadfield)
B. Boston's Nitro Line (Esposito, Hodge, Cashman)
C. Buffalo's French Connection (Perreault, Martin, Robert)
D. Los Angeles's Triple Crown Line (Dionne, Simmer, Taylor)

3.7 Who scored the first goal at both Toronto's Maple Leaf Gardens and Chicago Stadium?

A. Charlie Conacher
B. Joe Primeau
C. Dick Irvin
D. Harold "Mush" March

3.8 Who was the first player from a post-1967 expansion team to lead the NHL in playoff scoring?

A. Bill Goldsworthy of the 1968 Minnesota North Stars
B. Red Berenson of the 1971 St. Louis Blues
C. Rick MacLeish of the 1974 Philadelphia Flyers
D. Bryan Trottier of the 1980 New York Islanders

3.9 Which NHL team was the first to use a European-trained goalie?
A. The Quebec Nordiques
B. The New York Islanders
C. The Philadelphia Flyers
D. The Toronto Maple Leafs

3.10 In what decade did an NHL team first travel to a game by airplane?
A. 1920s
B. 1930s
C. 1940s
D. 1950s

3.11 Who was the first (and only) player to twice score three power-play goals in a playoff game?
A. Joe Sakic
B. Jari Kurri
C. Dino Ciccarelli
D. Michel Goulet

3.12 Which NHL arena hosted the first National Football League championship game?
A. Boston Garden
B. Chicago Stadium
C. Detroit's Olympia
D. New York's Madison Square Garden

3.13 Which was the first NHL team to put players' names on the back of their jerseys?
A. The Detroit Red Wings
B. The Montreal Canadiens
C. The Los Angeles Kings
D. The New York Americans

3.14 Which was the first NHL team to win the Stanley Cup with an American-born coach?
A. The Montreal Canadiens
B. The New York Rangers
C. The Chicago Blackhawks
D. The Pittsburgh Penguins

3.15 Which Toronto Maple Leafs player was the first defenseman to win the Calder Trophy as top rookie?
A. Allan Stanley
B. Kent Douglas
C. Carl Brewer
D. Wally Stanowski

3.16 Who was the first player of Asian ancestry to play in the NHL?
A. Jim Paek
B. Steve Tsujiura
C. Larry Kwong
D. Paul Kariya

3.17 The first NHLer born outside Canada to skate for a Stanley Cup champion came from what country?
A. USA
B. England
C. Russia
D. Australia

FIRST LIGHT
Answers

3.1 B. Bobby Orr
The offensive revolution began with No. 4. "All Bobby did," noted longtime Boston Bruins' teammate Phil Esposito, "was change the face of hockey all by himself." In 1969–70, Orr

became the first NHL defenseman, and only the fourth player, to crack the 100-point barrier, collecting 33 goals and 87 assists. That was the first of six straight 100-point seasons for the Bruins' golden boy, whose scoring barrage was finally halted by a knee injury just before the 1975–76 season. Even so, Orr was still a tough act to follow. Wayne Gretzky, with 13, is the only player to record more consecutive 100-point campaigns. Esposito, who, in 1968–69, became the first player to break 100 points, missed the 100-point mark by one point in 1969–70, preventing what otherwise would have been a string of seven straight century seasons.

3.2   C. England
Finland's Jari Kurri is often credited with being the first non-Canadian to score 50 goals, a milestone he topped in 1983–84 with the Edmonton Oilers, but Kurri was actually the second player with a foreign passport to do it. The first was Boston Bruins right-winger Ken Hodge, who scored 50 on the nose in 1973–74. Although raised in Canada, Hodge was born in Birmingham, England.

3.3   C. New York
Contrary to what Canadians believe, televised coverage of NHL games actually began in the U.S. As Brian McFarlane notes in his book *The Rangers,* the first hockey telecast took place in New York City on February 15, 1940. The game, between the Montreal Canadiens and the Rangers, was shown on an experimental station set up by NBC. It did not a have a large viewing audience, as there were only about 300 TV sets in the city. In fact, it was one of the rare times in history that the live audience at a sporting event outnumbered the one watching on TV. The CBC can't even claim credit for being the first station to regularly broadcast NHL games. During the 1946–47 season, the Chicago Blackhawks began televising their home games to a local market on station WBKB. The CBC did not launch its TV coverage until the 1952–53 season.

3.4 A. Sergei Fedorov
They say that speed kills. In that case Fedorov qualifies as a serial killer. The Detroit Red Wings centre, who had won the fastest-skater category at the All-Star skills competition in 1992 and 1994, added another notch to his stick by winning the hardest-shot category at the 2002 All-Star shindig. The talented Russian registered a 101.5 MPH howler to become the first player to capture both events.

3.5 C. 41
You can't say that goalie Hugh Lehman lacked postseason experience before starting his first NHL playoff game in 1927. The 41-year-old had already made five appearances in the Stanley Cup finals with the Vancouver Millionaires of the Pacific Coast Hockey Association, and had actually won the Cup in 1915. Even so, when Lehman stepped between the pipes for the Chicago Blackhawks in the 1927 quarterfinals against Boston, technically speaking, he became the oldest rookie to appear in an NHL playoff game. The Bruins gave Lehman a rough ride, beating the Hawks 6–1.

3.6 D. Los Angeles's Triple Crown Line (Dionne, Simmer, Taylor)
The line was assembled by Kings coach Bob Berry during the 1979–80 season. The trio clicked immediately with Marcel Dionne at centre, acting as the puck carrier and prime playmaker; Dave Taylor on right wing, playing the role of the mucker; and Charlie Simmer on left wing, as the triggerman. In 1980–81, the line made history by becoming the first NHL unit with three 100-point men: Dionne collected 135 points, Taylor, 122 and Simmer, 105.

3.7 D. Harold "Mush" March
The five-foot-five, 155-pound March, who was nicknamed after a cartoon character, scored the inaugural goals at two of the Original Six stadiums. The Chicago Blackhawks winger's first

brush with history came on November 21, 1929, when he scored the first goal at Chicago Stadium against Alex Connell in a 6–5 loss to the Ottawa Senators. Two years later, on November 12, 1931, March scored the first goal at Maple Leaf Gardens against netminder Lorne Chabot in a 2–1 Blackhawks' triumph over Toronto. But the biggest goal of March's career came on April 10, 1934, when he netted the overtime winner that gave Chicago its first Stanley Cup. March, who died at age 93 in January 2002, received a final tribute on the opening day of the 2001–02 season, when he dropped the puck for the ceremonial opening face-off at Chicago's new United Center.

3.8 A. Bill Goldsworthy of the 1968 Minnesota North Stars
Surprisingly, it was in 1967–68, the first year of expansion, that a player from an expansion team led the NHL in playoff scoring. Even odder, the player came from the Minnesota North Stars, a team that failed to make the finals. Bill Goldsworthy collected 15 points in 14 games to pace all playoff scorers. The top scorer on the Cup-champion Montreal Canadiens that year was Yvan Cournoyer with 14 points.

3.9 B. The New York Islanders
The first European-trained goalie to don the pads in the NHL was Sweden's Goran Hogosta, who made his debut on November 1, 1977, for the New York Islanders against the Atlanta Flames. Hogosta replaced an injured Billy Smith and played nine minutes, getting credit for a shared shutout in the Isles' 9–0 win. After his relief stint, Hogosta did not make another NHL appearance until 1979–80, when he played 21 games for the Quebec Nordiques.

3.10 A. 1920s
Although air travel did not become a common mode of transportation for NHL teams until the 1960s, the New York Rangers made history in December 1929, when club president, Colonel John Hammond, hired the Curtis-Wright Corporation to trans-

port the team to Toronto via airplane. Hammond was clearly not a superstitious man: the plane left on Friday the 13th. Flying didn't help the Blueshirts. They lost 7–6.

3.11 C. Dino Ciccarelli
Ciccarelli's name isn't one of the first that comes to mind when the topic is great scorers. But you will find him listed 12th on the all-time list, with 608 goals, ahead of such legends as Guy Lafleur and Stan Mikita. Ciccarelli's knack around the net was most evident in the postseason, where his 34 power-play goals ranks second only to Mike Bossy's 35. On April 29, 1993, with Detroit, Ciccarelli scored three times against Toronto in Game 6 of the division semifinals to become the ninth player in history to score a hat trick in a playoff game. On May 11, 1995, the feisty little winger duplicated the feat in a quarterfinals game against the Dallas Stars. That made Ciccarelli the first and only NHLer to notch two power-play hat tricks in the playoffs.

3.12 B. Chicago Stadium
When a raging snowstorm struck the state of Illinois in December 1932, National Football League officials decided that it would be impossible to play its championship game between the Chicago Bears and the Portsmouth Spartans on an outdoor field. The solution was to stage the game at Chicago Stadium, the home of the Blackhawks. Trucks dumped a layer of soil over the arena floor and crude line markings were painted over the surface. Because the field was only 80 yards long, every time a team crossed mid-field, it was put back 20 yards. More than 11,000 fans turned out for the contest, which was played on December 18, 1932. The Bears won the historic encounter 9–0. Chicago Stadium remains the only NHL rink used for an NFL game.

3.13 D. The New York Americans
The Americans' management adopted an aggressive and unconventional approach to marketing after the club joined the NHL in

1925. The between-periods entertainment at home games included barrel-jumping contests and dogsled races. In 1926, the Americans put player's names on the backs of their flashy coloured jerseys, a first in pro sports, and an innovation that the NHL didn't make mandatory until the 1970s.

3.14 A. The Montreal Canadiens

Strange, but true. The Montreal Canadiens, perhaps the team most closely identified with Canadian hockey, was the first NHL club to win the Stanley Cup with an American coach. The year was 1924 and the coach was Leo Dandurand, a native of Bourbonnais, Illinois. Dandurand moved to Canada in 1905, and later served as referee in the National Hockey Association, the predecessor to the NHL. One of the top sports entrepreneurs of his day, Dandurand was also the director of the Montreal Royals baseball team and the founder of the Montreal Alouettes football team. He bought the Canadiens with two partners in 1921 for US$11,000 and coached the club from 1921 to 1926, then again in 1934–35, before selling the team.

3.15 B. Kent Douglas

The Calder Trophy for the NHL's outstanding rookie was first presented in 1933. Thirty years elapsed before a defenseman won the award. During that time, several rookie rearguards were runner-ups, including Toronto's Wally Stanowski, Allan Stanley and Carl Brewer. It was not until 1963 that Douglas broke the drought. He played 70 games for Toronto in 1962–63, posting 22 points on seven goals and 15 assists as the Leafs captured the Cup. The previous year, Douglas had won the Eddie Shore Award as the top defenseman in the American Hockey League. Despite his impressive start, Douglas never developed into an elite rearguard and, unlike the other three Leafs who were Calder Trophy runner-ups, he was never elected to an NHL All-Star team.

3.16 C. Larry Kwong

The son of a Chinese grocer from Vernon, British Columbia, Larry Kwong grew up dreaming of one day skating in the NHL. After a long slog through the minors, he finally got his shot and was called up by the injury riddled New York Rangers for an encounter against the Canadiens at the Montreal Forum. The date was March 13, 1948. The right-winger's stay with the big club was painfully brief. He played just one shift in the game, and then was returned to the New York Rovers of the Eastern Hockey League. Kwong later played for the Valleyfield Braves of the Quebec Senior League, where he thrived under coach Toe Blake, winning the league's MVP award in 1950–51 and leading the club to the senior title. But after his one New York minute, he never got another crack at the big time.

3.17 A. USA

The lineup of the Toronto Arenas, winners of the Stanley Cup in the NHL's first season, 1917–18, was composed almost entirely of Canadians. In fact, 12 of the club's 13 players were born in Ontario. The lone exception was defenseman Harry Mummery from Chicago, Illinois. Mummery, who stood five-foot-eleven and weighed 220 pounds, was not only one of the largest players of the era, but also an effective playmaker. During the 1918 eastern playoffs against Montreal, he scored a goal. Then, in the Cup finals against Vancouver, he posted six assists, giving him two more distinctions: the first non-Canadian to score a goal in the playoffs and the first to record a point in the Cup finals.

Game 3

THE FIRST FIVE-TEAM 20-GOAL MAN

Who was the first NHLer to record 20-goal seasons with five different teams? Most of the players listed below have scored 20 goals with at least two different clubs, some have done it with three, others, such as Doug Gilmour, with four teams and a select few, such as Eddie Shack and Mike Gartner, are five-team 20-goal men. Their names, such as Adam OATES, appear in the puzzle horizontally, vertically, diagonally or backwards. After you've circled all 45 words, read the remaining letters in descending order to spell our unknown shooter. As a bonus we've circled a few words, including FIVE and TEAMS and the first name of our mystery 20-goal man, DEAN.

(*Solutions are on page 119*)

Amonte	Arnott	Bathgate	Bure
Carson	Clark	Coffey	Dean
Dionne	Esposito	Five	Francis
Gartner	Gilmour	Goulet	Gretzky
Guerin	Hull	Kovalev	Kurri
Larionov	MacInnis	Messier	Mogilny
Mullen	Muller	Murphy	Nicholls
Nolan	Oates	Palffy	Recchi
Robitaille	Roenick	Selanne	Shack
Stastny	Shanahan	Sundin	Teams
Turgeon	Yashin	Zhamnov	Nieuwendyk
Andreychuk			

```
A O T I S O P S E N O E G R U T S
N N I C H O L L S I T E L U O G E
I T D R E N O G R E T Z K Y P I L
D E Y R R N A A M U L L E R M L A
N A E O E U N L T W R L L U H M N
U M F B G Y K O O E E N R S L O N
S S F I U T C Z I N S P H A I U E
Y I O T E Y R H B D H A R B K R V
N N C A R N E A U Y C I A O F N I
L N A I I T N M R K O T V R R A F
I I R L N S T N E N H A A E O H N
G C S L A A R O O G L N C T E A I
O A O E E T A V A E C C L N N N H
M M N C D S G T V I H E A O I A S
N E L L U M E S S I E R R M C H A
Y F F L A P T T O N R A K A K S Y
```

4

DYNASTY ROW

What constitutes a hockey dynasty? There is no hard-and-fast rule, but many insist that a team has to capture three Stanley Cups in a row to qualify. As Steve Yzerman once noted: "Good teams win one, outstanding teams win two and a few truly great teams win three." Still, that definition would exclude the Edmonton Oilers, who won four Cups in five years in the 1980s, but not three in a row. While you consider that question, we'll fire some more your way on the subject of great teams.

(*Answers are on page 46*)

4.1 Which club holds the record for most consecutive first-place finishes?
   A. The Montreal Canadiens
   B. The Detroit Red Wings
   C. The Edmonton Oilers
   D. The New York Islanders

4.2 Which is the only NHL team to score 200 more goals than it allowed in a season?
   A. The 1970–71 Boston Bruins
   B. The 1976–77 Montreal Canadiens
   C. The 1984–85 Edmonton Oilers
   D. The 1995–96 Detroit Red Wings

4.3 Of all the Stanley Cup-winning teams, which one had the most future Hall of Famers in its lineup?
   A. The 1952 Detroit Red Wings
   B. The 1956 Montreal Canadiens
   C. The 1967 Toronto Maple Leafs
   D. The 1973 Montreal Canadiens

4.4 In 1962, the Boston Bruins secured the cornerstone of a dynasty when they bought the lifetime hockey rights to Bobby Orr. How much was the contract worth?
A. US$2,800
B. US$6,800
C. US$24,800
D. US$50,800

4.5 Which dynasty holds the record for winning the most consecutive playoff series?
A. The 1950s Montreal Canadiens
B. The 1970s Montreal Canadiens
C. The 1980s New York Islanders
D. The 1980s Edmonton Oilers

4.6 Which of the following playoff records set by the 1985 Edmonton Oilers has since been surpassed?
A. Most goals in one playoff game
B. Most goals in one playoff series
C. Most shorthanded goals in one playoff year
D. Most three-or-more goals in one playoff year

4.7 Which team led the NHL in goals scored for the most consecutive seasons?
A. The Maurice Richard–Jean Béliveau era Montreal Canadiens
B. The Bobby Hull–Stan Mikita era Chicago Blackhawks
C. The Bobby Orr–Phil Esposito era Boston Bruins
D. The Wayne Gretzky–Mark Messier era Edmonton Oilers

4.8 Which Cup-winning coach was a great admirer of the Russian hockey system and once even travelled to Moscow to take a course taught by Soviet national coach Anatoly Tarasov?

A. Al Arbour of the New York Islanders
B. Fred Shero of the Philadelphia Flyers
C. Scotty Bowman of the Montreal Canadiens
D. Glen Sather of the Edmonton Oilers

4.9 How many players from the Toronto Maple Leafs 1966–67 Stanley Cup-winning squad finished in the top 20 regular-season scorers?

A. Two players
B. Four players
C. Six players
D. Eight players

4.10 Which is the only team in NHL history to score 100 more goals than any other team in the league?

A. The 1970–71 Boston Bruins
B. The 1976–77 Montreal Canadiens
C. The 1983–84 Edmonton Oilers
D. The 1992–93 Pittsburgh Penguins

4.11 Which 1990s team posted the largest single-season improvement in points in NHL history?

A. The 1992–93 Quebec Nordiques
B. The 1993–94 San Jose Sharks
C. The 1996–97 Dallas Stars
D. The 1998–99 Toronto Maple Leafs

4.12 Montreal and Boston have one of hockey's great rivalries. But for much of the 20th century, it was a one-sided affair. How many consecutive playoff series did Montreal take from Boston between 1946 and 1988?

A. Nine consecutive series
B. 12 consecutive series
C. 15 consecutive series
D. 18 consecutive series

4.13 The Philadelphia Flyers went undefeated a record 35 consecutive games in 1979–80. Who coached the Flyers that season?

A. Fred Shero
B. Pat Quinn
C. Bob McCammon
D. Mike Keenan

4.14 What is the NHL record for most consecutive shutouts by a team to start a season?

A. Two games
B. Three games
C. Five games
D. Seven games

4.15 Which regular-season champion finished a record 27 points ahead of the second-place team?

A. The 1943–44 Montreal Canadiens
B. The 1977–78 Montreal Canadiens
C. The 1983–84 Edmonton Oilers
D. The 1995–96 Detroit Red Wings

4.16 Which was last Canadian senior amateur team to win the World Championships?
  A. The Whitby Dunlops
  B. The Chatham Maroons
  C. The Penticton Vees
  D. The Trail Smoke Eaters

4.17 Which team owns the record for scoring the most power-play goals in a season?
  A. The 1971–72 Boston Bruins
  B. The 1983–84 Edmonton Oilers
  C. The 1988–89 Pittsburgh Penguins
  D. The 1995–96 Detroit Red Wings

4.18 The Edmonton Oilers set the standard for most goals in a season in 1983–84. How many goals did they score?
  A. 399 goals
  B. 423 goals
  C. 446 goals
  D. 467 goals

DYNASTY ROW
Answers

4.1   B. The Detroit Red Wings
The Gordie Howe-led Detroit teams of the early 1950s were a formidable force. Detroit finished at the top of the NHL a record seven straight seasons from 1948–49 to 1954–55, winning four Stanley Cups. As outstanding as these achievements are, had the Wings played up to their potential they could have won more. As the playoff favourites, the Motor City boys were upset in three separate series, each one costing them the championship. In the 1949 finals the Wings fell to the fourth-place Maple Leafs, a club that finished 18 points behind them in the standings. They were

also surprised in the 1951 semifinals by the third-place Canadiens, who finished 36 points behind them, and in the 1953 semifinals by the third-place Bruins, who were 21 points back. The "what-ifs" are easy, but count for nothing. On paper the Red Wings should have had seven Cups in a row.

4.2 **B. The 1976–77 Montreal Canadiens**
Many believe that the Montreal teams of the late 1970s formed the most awesome dynasty of all time. The chart below supports that claim. The 1976–77 Canadiens squad was a juggernaut. Guy Lafleur, Larry Robinson, Ken Dryden and company posted a 60–8–12 mark and amassed an NHL-record 132 points. The team's dominance is reflected in its goals-for and goals-against numbers. The Habs scored 387 times, while allowing opponents only 171, a difference of 216. That's 24 goals better than the closest team, the 1970–71 Boston Bruins.

LARGEST GOAL-DIFFERENTIALS IN A SEASON

Team	Season	GF	GA	Margin
Montreal	1976–77	387	171	216
Boston	1970–71	399	207	192
Montreal	1977–78	359	183	176
Montreal	1975–76	337	174	163
Montreal	1974–75	374	225	149
Montreal	1972–73	329	184	145

4.3 **D. The 1973 Montreal Canadiens**
Although it's rarely cited as one of the greatest teams of all time, this Montreal Stanley Cup winner had a record 11 future Hall of Famers on its roster. The list includes Ken Dryden, Serge Savard, Larry Robinson, Guy Lapointe, Jacques Laperriere, Guy Lafleur, Steve Shutt, Henri Richard, Frank Mahovlich, Yvan Cournoyer and Jacques Lemaire.

4.4   A. US$2,800

Fourteen-year-old Bobby Orr signed the standard NHL "C" form, which gave the Boston Bruins his hockey rights for life in exchange for US$2,800, a used car and the promise of a new wardrobe (the Bruins never did deliver the new wardrobe). In 1966, when Orr tuned pro, agent Alan Eagleson negotiated a more lucrative deal for his client. Orr inked the largest rookie contract ever seen at that time in the NHL: US$80,000 over two years, including a US$25,000 signing bonus. Money was never better spent.

4.5   C. The 1980s New York Islanders

During the Islanders' glory years, they captured four straight Stanley Cups and 19 straight playoff series. It's a record of sustained excellence that may never be broken. The closest contender is the Montreal Canadiens, who won 13 straight series from 1976 to 1980. The Isles' reign began in 1980, when they opened the playoffs with a three-games-to-one triumph over the Los Angeles Kings. The string continued until the 1984 finals when the Islanders were dethroned by the Edmonton Oilers, four games to one.

4.6   A. Most goals in one playoff game

It's difficult to decide which Edmonton Oilers team of the 1980s was the most explosive; they all had supersonic weaponry. But during the 1985 playoffs, opposition goalies got radiation burns on the backs of their necks from the repeated flashing of the red light. That spring, Wayne Gretzky set a new record for most points (47) in one playoff year; Jari Kurri set a record for most hat tricks (four) in one playoff year; and Paul Coffey set a record for points (37) by a defenseman in one playoff year. The Oilers also bagged team records for most goals in a series (44 against Chicago in the conference finals); most shorthanded goals in one playoff year (10 in 16 games); and most players scoring hat tricks in one playoff year (six). The 11 goals that the Oilers scored against

Chicago in Game 1 of the conference finals (equalling Montreal's 1944 record), is one of the few records they set that did not survive. It was broken in 1987 by another Oilers club that pumped in a baker's dozen in a 13–3 massacre of Los Angeles in the division semifinals.

4.7   A. The Maurice Richard–Jean Béliveau era Montreal Canadiens
The 1950s may not have been a high-scoring decade, but you would have had trouble convincing the rest of the NHL that the Canadiens lacked firepower. Beginning in 1953–54, the Habs embarked on an amazing record streak of 10 straight seasons as the NHL's top scoring team. As a point of reference to Montreal's dominance, the Wayne Gretzky–Mark Messier era Edmonton Oilers, hockey's highest scoring club, strung together only six successive regular seasons as the league's best scorers. By the time Montreal's run ended in 1963–64, the Flying Frenchmen had added five Stanley Cups to their trophy case.

4.8   B. Fred Shero of the Philadelphia Flyers
Although Shero was the architect who put together the infamous brawling Flyers teams of the mid-1970s, he had long been a student and admirer of the Russian game. Just weeks after he coached Philadelphia to its first Stanley Cup in May 1974, Shero attended a three-week course in Moscow on sport and physical education conducted by Soviet national coach Anatoly Tarasov. However, few, if any, of Tarasov's theories were ever employed by Shero with the Flyers, whose approach to hockey he once candidly described as "controlled mayhem."

4.9   A. Two players
Common wisdom around the NHL in 1966–67 dictated that the Toronto Maple Leafs dynasty of the early 1960s was long over. With an average age of 31, the Maple Leafs were considered too old to make another serious run at a championship. Toronto's

offense certainly didn't scare anyone. Only two Leaf players—Dave Keon at 12th and Frank Mahovlich at 19th—placed among the top 20 point earners. Of the twenty 20-goal scorers in the league that season, just two were Leafs: Ron Ellis with 22 goals and Jim Pappin with 21. But Toronto's veteran crew could play solid defense, and with goalies Terry Sawchuk and Johnny Bower holding the fort, the club upset favourites Chicago and Montreal to capture the Stanley Cup.

4.10 A. 1970–71 Boston Bruins
The transformation of the Bruins from league doormat to league powerhouse was triggered by the arrival of Bobby Orr in 1966–67, and the acquisition of Phil Esposito, Ken Hodge and Fred Stanfield in a one-sided deal with Chicago prior to the 1967–68 season. The Big Bad Bruins put the fear into everyone, especially at Boston Garden where they stomped opponents with malicious zeal. The most explosive Boston team of the era was the 1970–71 edition, which scored 399 goals, 108 more than any other team in the league that season. Not even the high-flying Edmonton Oilers teams of the 1980s could match that margin of domination.

LARGEST MARGIN IN GOALS SCORED

Teams	Season	Goals	Margin
Boston Bruins	1970–71	399	108
Montreal Canadiens		291	
Edmonton Oilers	1983–84	446	89
New York Islanders		357	
Edmonton Oilers	1982–83	424	74
Montreal Canadiens		350	
Edmonton Oilers	1985–86	426	72
Calgary Flames		354	

4.11 B. The 1993–94 San Jose Sharks

Under rookie coach Kevin Constantine, San Jose made the playoffs for the first time in 1993–94, improving its 1992–93 record by 58 points, jumping from 24 to 82 points. The dramatic turnaround eclipsed the 52-point leap by the 1992–93 Quebec Nordiques as the largest single-season improvement in NHL history. The Sharks' surge was sparked by the crafty play of veteran forwards Igor Larionov and Sergei Makarov, the maturation of young defenseman Sandis Ozolinsh and the acrobatic netminding of Arturs Irbe. San Jose continued its inspired play in the postseason, upsetting top-seeded Detroit, before falling to Toronto in seven games.

4.12 D. 18 consecutive series

Montreal has defeated many teams in the playoffs, but no club has suffered so much at the hands of the Canadiens as the Bruins. Montreal's mysterious postseason mastery of Boston spanned 41 years and a record-setting 18 straight series. The streak began in 1946, when Rocket Richard and his mates defeated the Beantowners in the Cup finals. It continued up until 1988, when the Terry O'Reilly-coached Bruins finally subdued the Habs in five games in the Adams Division finals.

4.13 B. Pat Quinn

After losing to the Atlanta Flames in their second game of the 1979–80 season, the Flyers decided to get serious. Very serious. They went on a rampage, going 35 straight games without a loss, the longest undefeated streak in NHL history. Under the direction of coach Pat Quinn, the "Broad Street Bullies" changed their style, emphasizing speed and quickness, cutting back on the violence that had been the club's hallmark. Philadelphia finished the season with 116 points, the highest total in the league.

4.14 C. Five games

The Toronto Maple Leafs began the 1930–31 season by blanking their opponents in five straight games. After opening with a 0–0 draw on home ice against the New York Americans, Toronto stifled the Philadelphia Quakers 4–0. Then they headed out on the road and defeated the Montreal Canadiens 3–0, tied the Americans 0–0 and downed the Ottawa Senators 2–0. The Leafs' shutout streak ended in their next game in the City of Brotherly Love, when they were edged 2–1 by the Quakers. Philadelphia was an unlikely club to snap the streak: it won just four games all season and scored a league-low 76 goals in 44 games. After its fast start, Toronto posted only three more goose eggs the rest of the way. The Leafs ended the year ranked sixth best in goals allowed, finishing second in the Canadian Division behind the Montreal Canadiens.

4.15 D. The 1995–96 Detroit Red Wings

Scotty Bowman's Red Wings played superb hockey in 1995–96, racking up a record of 62–13–7. No other team has ever won more games or finished so far ahead of the competition. Detroit's 131 points was 27 points better than the second-place Colorado Avalanche. However, Colorado got the last laugh, upsetting Detroit in the Western Conference finals and going on to win the Stanley Cup. As good as the Red Wings were in 1995–96, in relative terms, the two teams that rank second and third on the all-time chart were even more dominant. In 1929–30, Boston finished 26 points ahead of the next-closest team in a 44-game schedule, and in 1943–44, Montreal had a 25-point cushion over the runner-up in a 50-game schedule.

4.16 D. The Trail Smoke Eaters

The last time a Canadian senior team won the World Championships was in Geneva, Switzerland, in 1961. Canada was represented by British Columbia's Trail Smoke Eaters. The Smokies entered the final game of the tournament needing to defeat the defending-champion Soviet Union by a margin of four goals to win the gold medal. A dramatic goal by Norm Lenardon late in the third period gave Canada a 5–1 victory and the 1961 world hockey title. Every member of this legendary Trail team was a hometown boy, except captain Cal Hockley, who came from nearby Fernie, B.C.

4.17 **C. The 1988–89 Pittsburgh Penguins**
The Penguins already had a dangerous power play thanks to the presence of Mario Lemieux, but when the club acquired defenseman Paul Coffey in a trade with Edmonton midway through the 1987–88 season, the unit moved up to another level. Pittsburgh waged a battle with the New York Rangers and Winnipeg Jets in 1987–88 for the NHL record for most goals with a man-advantage. The Rangers won, scoring 111 goals, while the Penguins and Jets counted 110. But the next season, with Coffey in the lineup from opening day, the Penguins scored 119 power-play goals, setting a record that has never been surpassed.

4.18 **C. 446 goals**
Score, score and score some more was the motto of the Oiler teams of the 1980s. Edmonton's troop of machine-gunners hit the target 417 times in 1981–82 to become the first NHL club to crack the 400-goal barrier. The next year, the Oilers pushed the mark to 424, and then in 1983–84 they raised the standard to an amazing 446 goals. Leading the goal-scoring charge that year were Wayne Gretzky (87), Glenn Anderson (54), Jari Kurri (52) and Paul Coffey (40). In all, Edmonton registered five 400-goal seasons from 1981–82 to 1985–86. That type of production now seems miraculous. No NHL team has topped 300 goals since 1995–96.

Game 4

NOT-WAYNE-GRETZKY-OFFENSIVE RECORDS

The holder of 61 NHL records, Wayne Gretzky practically owns the league's offensive records section. But a few scoring marks eluded the Great One during his career. Listed below are 10 players who managed to outscore the Great One in at least 10 different categories. Match these NHLers and their "not-Gretzky" records.

(Solutions are on page 119)

Mario Lemieux   ✗Darryl Sittler   Joe Malone
Mike Bossy   Bryan Trottier   Steve Thomas
Harry Broadbent   Mike Gartner   Tim Kerr
Dale Hawerchuk

1. _____Sittler_____ Most goals in one game

2. _____ Most power-play goals in one season

3. _____ Most shorthanded goals in one season

4. _____ Most overtime goals in a career

5. _____ Most assists in one period

6. _____ Most points in one game

7. _____ Most points in one period

8. _____ Most 30-or-more-goal seasons

9. _____ Most consecutive 50-or-more-goal seasons

10. _____ Longest consecutive goal-scoring streak

5
MASKED MARVELS

Ken Dryden was called "the Thinker" because of his habit of propping his chin on his goalie stick during lulls in the action, a pensive pose that was reminiscent of Rodin's famous sculpture of the same name. Phil Esposito gave the Montreal goalie another moniker. When the long-limbed rookie stonewalled the Boston Bruins in the 1971 playoffs, Espo called Dryden "a thieving giraffe." This chapter is dedicated to the thieving giraffes and other masked marvels who make their living keeping the puck out.

(*Answers are on page 58*)

5.1 Which team did Patrick Roy defeat in December 2001 to record his 500th career win?
A. The Montreal Canadiens
B. The New York Rangers
C. The Dallas Stars
D. The Toronto Maple Leafs

5.2 What does Phoenix Coyotes netminder Sean Burke have painted on his mask?
A. Images of rock guitarists
B. Images of fighter pilots
C. Images of rattlesnakes
D. Images of Roman gladiators

5.3 Which goaltender goes by the nickname "Moose"?
A. Dan Cloutier of the Vancouver Canucks
B. Johan Hedberg of the Pittsburgh Penguins
C. Brent Johnson of the St. Louis Blues
D. Roberto Luongo of the Florida Panthers

5.4 Who is the youngest goalie to play in the NHL?
   A. Frank Brimsek
   B. Terry Sawchuk
   C. Harry Lumley
   D. John Vanbiesbrouck

5.5 In 2001–02, who became the second-youngest goalie in NHL history to see action?
   A. Alex Auld of the Vancouver Canucks
   B. Jussi Markkanen of the Edmonton Oilers
   C. Dan Blackburn of the New York Rangers
   D. Olivier Michaud of the Montreal Canadiens

5.6 Which goaltender nearly died on the ice when his jugular vein was slashed by a skate blade?
   A. Clint Malarchuk
   B. Murray Bannerman
   C. Gilles Meloche
   D. Mike Palmateer

5.7 What is the fewest number of regular-season games played by a goalie before leading his team to a championship in the Stanley Cup finals?
   A. Zero games
   B. Six games
   C. 12 games
   D. 24 games

5.8 Which NHL goalkeeper went unbeaten in a record 32 straight games?
   A. Ken Dryden
   B. Bernie Parent
   C. Gerry Cheevers
   D. Pete Peeters

5.9 Who was the first European-trained goalie to start an
NHL game?
  A. Sweden's Hardy Astrom
  B. Czechoslovakia's Jiri Crha
  C. Finland's Markus Mattsson
  D. Sweden's Pelle Lindbergh

5.10 What piece of equipment, used by more than a dozen NHL
goalies, was made illegal after the 2000–01 season?
  A. An extra piece of webbing on the trapper
  B. The air-filled chest protector
  C. The hanging throat guard
  D. A small secondary skate blade

5.11 Including playoff games, which goaltender holds the NHL
record for playing in the most games during one season?
  A. Grant Fuhr
  B. Ed Belfour
  C. Ron Hextall
  D. Martin Brodeur

5.12 Which rookie goalie led the NHL in both goals-against average
and save percentage in 2000–01?
  A. Dallas's Marty Turco
  B. San Jose's Evgeni Nabokov
  C. Colorado's David Aebischer
  D. Philadelphia's Roman Cechmanek

5.13 Which goalie leases a luxury suite at his home arena for
seriously ill children?
  A. Sean Burke
  B. Martin Brodeur
  C. Olaf Kolzig
  D. Curtis Joseph

5.14 Who is the only modern-day goalie to post shutouts with six
different NHL teams?

A. Sean Burke
B. Bob Essensa
C. Grant Fuhr
D. Gary Smith

5.15 Who holds the record for the highest save-percentage in
a season?

A. Gump Worsley of the 1962–63 New York Rangers
B. Jacques Plante of the 1970–71 Toronto Maple Leafs
C. Curtis Joseph of the 1992–93 St. Louis Blues
D. Dominik Hasek of the 1998–99 Buffalo Sabres

5.16 What is the NHL record for most consecutive shutouts by
a goalie?

A. Four shutouts
B. Five shutouts
C. Six shutouts
D. Seven shutouts

5.17 Who led the NHL in shutouts a record seven seasons?

A. Alex Connell
B. Clint Benedict
C. Glenn Hall
D. Terry Sawchuk

MASKED MARVELS
Answers

5.1 C. The Dallas Stars

Patrick Roy notched win No. 500 in classic style, blanking Dallas
2–0, on December 26, 2001. The Colorado ace stopped 31 shots
for the 59th shutout of his career. "He's the best goalie in the

world, the best ever—that's what 500 wins means," said Avalanche defenseman Rob Blake. "It's an honour to play with him." The first person to congratulate Roy was his 10-year-old son, Frederick, who was waiting at the exit gate when his father skated off the ice.

5.2 A. Images of rock guitarists
An avid guitarist himself, Burke used to wear a mask adorned with portraits of rock legends Jimi Hendrix and Jimmy Page. In keeping with the theme, he recently introduced a new model that features Eddie Van Halen and Slash, the lead guitarist from the band Guns N' Roses. Burke says that the images on masks are an expression of a goalie's personality. "It's not like every other position, where everybody's wearing the same thing. Masks are a lot cooler now. It's an art form."

5.3 B. Johan Hedberg of the Pittsburgh Penguins
How does a five-foot-eleven, 185-pound Swedish goalie come to be called "Moose"? Because he used to be one, that's how. Hedberg spent most of the 2000–01 season tending goal for the Manitoba Moose of the International Hockey League. The goalie mask he wore for Manitoba was a sky-blue colour with a moose painted on it. On March 12, 2001, the Penguins acquired Hedberg in a trade with San Jose, and brought him up for a tryout. The 27-year-old with the distinctive head gear was sensational, losing only one of nine games to close out the season. Pittsburgh fans began chanting "Mooooose!" every time he made a save. The Winnipeg team's Web site was swamped by fans searching for souvenir moose antlers and Hedberg's game-worn jerseys. The rookie continued his roll in the postseason, leading Pittsburgh to victories over Washington and Buffalo, before New Jersey ended the Moose's Cinderella run.

5.4 C. Harry Lumley
Unless the NHL changes its rules regarding the age of draft picks, this record is set in stone. On December 19, 1943, Lumley

donned the pads with the Detroit Red Wings at the age of 17 years, 38 days, losing 6–2 to the New York Rangers. Lumley played one more game with the Wings, a 7–1 loss to Chicago, before being sent down to the Indianapolis Capitols of the Central Hockey League. He would win the starting job the next year. Oddly, during his brief tryout in 1943, Lumley, on loan from Detroit, also played for the New York Rangers, subbing in the third period for injured Ken McAuley in a game against his own team. That earned Lumley another distinction: the youngest goalie to play for two NHL teams.

5.5   D. Olivier Michaud of the Montreal Canadiens
Although no one has seriously threatened Harry Lumley's record as the youngest netminder to play in the NHL, Olivier Michaud came the closest of any, debuting with the Canadiens at the age of 18 years and 46 days, on October 30, 2001. Michaud, who was on loan from the Shawinigan Cataractes of the Quebec Junior League, replaced Mathieu Garon for the third period of a 3–1 loss to the Edmonton Oilers, and stopped all 14 shots he faced. Until Michaud's appearance, John Vanbiesbrouck, who was 18 years and 93 days old when he saw action with the New York Rangers on December 15, 1981, was the second youngest. Vanbiesbrouck, who beat the Colorado Rockies 2–1 in his debut, remains the youngest goalie to post a win in his first NHL game.

5.6   A. Clint Malarchuk
It was one of the most horrific injuries in NHL history. On March 22, 1989, Buffalo Sabres goalie Clint Malarchuk was involved in a collision with St. Louis Blues rookie Steve Tuttle and Buffalo's Uwe Krupp. Tuttle's skate blade sliced a six-inch gash in Malarchuk's throat. Blood gushed from the wound. Aware he was in serious trouble, the Sabres' goalie clutched his throat and skated frantically to the bench. "I thought I was dying," Malarchuk said. "I knew it was my jugular vein and I didn't have long to live." The team's trainer and doctor controlled the bleeding with pressure

and gauze, then rushed the stricken goalie to the hospital. Incredibly, Malarchuk was back in the Sabres' net 11 days later, with 300 stitches.

5.7   A. Zero games
Many mistakenly believe this record belongs to Ken Dryden, who played only six regular-season games with the Montreal Canadiens before leading them to the Stanley Cup in 1971. However, rookie goaltender Earl Robertson didn't play a single regular-season game in 1936–37, before he backstopped the Detroit Red Wings to the Cup. Robertson was called up from the minors when starter Normie Smith's injured arm prevented him from playing in the finals against the New York Rangers. Robertson played like a bandit, blanking the Rangers 1–0 and 3–0 in the last two games as Detroit rallied to win the best-of-five series in five games. Oddly, Robertson never played a single regular-season game for the Red Wings in his career. Two weeks after winning the Cup, he was traded to the New York Americans.

5.8   C. Gerry Cheevers
The Boston Bruins of the early 1970s were famed for their blitzkrieg offense and smashmouth physical play, but an overlooked ingredient of the Bruins' success was their goaltending. Gerry Cheevers may not have put up flashy shutout or goals-against numbers, but no one was better at making clutch saves with the game on the line. As he once admitted: "I don't care much about my average. My philosophy has always been that the other team can fill the net on me as long as we get one more goal." In 1971–72, Cheevers went unbeaten in 32 straight games (24 wins, eight ties) and helped lead Boston to the league title and its second Stanley Cup in three years. The next year he jumped ship to play in the WHA, and the Bruins crashed and burned in the quarterfinals.

LONGEST UNDEFEATED STREAK BY A GOALIE

Goalie	Team	Season	Streak
Gerry Cheevers	Boston	1971–72	32 games
Pete Peeters	Boston	1982–83	31 games
Pete Peeters	Philadelphia	1979–80	27 games
Frank Brimsek	Boston	1940–41	23 games
Chico Resch	NY Islanders	1978–79	23 games
Grant Fuhr	Edmonton	1981–82	23 games

5.9 **A. Sweden's Hardy Astrom**

On February 25, 1978, New York Rangers coach Jean-Guy Talbot played a desperate hunch and gave Swedish rookie Hardy Astrom the starting assignment against the Canadiens at the Montreal Forum. No goalie has ever had a more intimidating NHL debut. The Canadiens, one of the mightiest teams of all time, were riding an NHL record 28-game unbeaten streak, and the Rangers had not won a game at the Forum in six seasons. For Astrom, the occasion was doubly significant: he was the first European netminder to start an NHL game. Overcoming the odds, he played brilliantly, sparking the Rangers to a 6–3 victory. Unfortunately for Astrom, it was one of the rare highlights in an otherwise undistinguished career. He saw action in only three more games for the Rangers, and was later traded to the woeful Colorado Rockies. There, he played two miserable years for coach Don Cherry, who took delight in heaping abuse on the European, calling Astrom "my Swedish sieve."

5.10 **D. A small secondary skate blade**

The device, a small piece of sharpened metal that attaches to the bottom of a goalie's skate boot to improve traction, had been used by NHL netminders since 1996–97. The blade gave goalies greater mobility because they could use it to push off while on their knees—even when their main skate blade was off the ice. NHL general managers banned the blade after the 2000–01 season, ruling it was a performance-enhancing device rather than a protective piece of equipment.

5.11   D.   Martin Brodeur
Brodeur broke Grant Fuhr's 94-game mark from the 1987–88 season when he backstopped the New Jersey Devils to a Stanley Cup championship on June 10, 2000. It was Brodeur's 95th game of the season. In 2000–01, Brodeur snapped his own record by appearing in 72 regular-season games and 25 playoff matches, a total of 97 games between the pipes.

MOST GAMES BY A GOALIE IN ONE SEASON, INCLUDING PLAYOFFS *

Goalie	Team	Season	RS	P	Total
Martin Brodeur	New Jersey	2000–01	72	25	97
Martin Brodeur	New Jersey	1999–2000	72	23	95
Grant Fuhr	Edmonton	1987–88	75	19	94
Ron Hextall	Philadelphia	1986–87	66	26	92
Mike Richter	NY Rangers	1993–94	68	23	91

* Current to 2001–02

5.12   A.   Dallas's Marty Turco
Goalie Ed Belfour's erratic behaviour off the ice and his clashes with Dallas coach Ken Hitchcock led to increased ice time for backup Marty Turco in 2000–01, and the freshman responded by posting sterling numbers. In 26 games, Turco led all goalies with a 1.90 GAA and a .925 save percentage, a double-first for a rookie netminder.

5.13 D. Curtis Joseph

When he was a member of the Edmonton Oilers, Joseph and his wife, Nancy, began inviting kids from the local Sick Children's hospital to the arena to watch a game from a private suite. After Joseph joined the Toronto Maple Leafs in 1998, he and his wife continued the program. As part of his contract, Joseph leases a CDN$100,000 luxury suite at Toronto's Air Canada Centre. Each home game, 16 children suffering from cancer and other serious illnesses are selected from local hospitals to use the box. After the game, the Leafs goalie often visits with them and signs sticks, sweaters and posters.

5.14 A. Sean Burke

In 1999–2000, Burke joined old-timer Lorne Chabot as the only two netminders to register shutouts with six NHL teams. Chabot logged zeroes with each of the six teams he played for: the New York Rangers, Toronto Maple Leafs, Chicago Blackhawks, Montreal Canadiens, Montreal Maroons and New York Americans. Burke has posted goose eggs with six of the seven teams he has played for: the New Jersey Devils, Hartford Whalers, Carolina Hurricanes, Philadelphia Flyers, Florida Panthers and Phoenix Coyotes. Burke did not earn a shutout with the Vancouver Canucks in the 16 games he played for the club in 1997–98.

5.15 B. Jacques Plante of the 1970–71 Toronto Maple Leafs

Although Plante is best remembered for his stellar work with the Montreal Canadiens in the late 1950s, he was just as spectacular when he returned to the NHL after a three-year retirement in the late 1960s. Plante led the league in goals-against average in 1968–69 with the St. Louis Blues and did it again with Toronto in 1970–71. His play for a mediocre Maple Leaf team, at age 41, was remarkable. That season, Plante posted a .942 save percentage, the best in recorded history. His impact can be gauged by examining Toronto's record. The Leafs were 24–11–4 with Jake the Snake in the net, and 13–22–4 without him. Based on his workload, Dominik Hasek, who ranks second in the category with a .937 save percentage for the Buffalo Sabres in 1998–99, may have turned in the most impressive season by a goalie of all time. Hasek logged 24 more games and faced 612 more shots than Plante did in 1970–71.

Highest Single-Season Save Percentages*

Goalie	Team	Season	GP	Shots	SPCT
Jacques Plante	Toronto	1970–71	40	1,265	.942
Dominik Hasek	Buffalo	1998–99	64	1,877	.937
Johnny Bower	Toronto	1963–64	51	1,587	.933
Dominik Hasek	Buffalo	1997–98	72	2,149	.932

* since 1954–55

5.16 C. Six shutouts

For six straight games in 1927–28, Ottawa Senators netminder Alex Connell was unbeatable. With Connell holding the fort, the Senators beat the Toronto Maple Leafs 4–0, the Montreal Maroons 1–0, then posted three scoreless ties, two against the New York Rangers and one against the Pittsburgh Pirates, before edging the Montreal Canadiens 1–0. Finally, at 15:50 during the second period of the seventh game of the streak, Chicago Blackhawks forward Duke Keats put a puck past Connell. The final tally was 461 minutes, 29 seconds of shutout hockey.

5.17 B. Clint Benedict

Benedict paced the NHL in shutouts for seven straight seasons with the Ottawa Senators from 1917–18 to 1923–24. The most zeroes he recorded in one season during that span were five, in 1919–20. Although Benedict logged far more shutouts in his last six seasons than in his first seven—41 as opposed to 17—he did not lead the NHL again, as offense declined in the late 1920s and double-digit shutout totals became common.

Game 5

BLOODLINES

The game of hockey has produced more than 70 father-and-son combinations and at least 200 brothers have appeared in the NHL. Listed below are the first names of fathers, sons and brothers from 22 hockey families. Once you figure out their family names from their first-name combinations, find them in the puzzle by reading across, down or diagonally. Following our example of Chris and Sean PRONGER, connect the family names using letters no more than once. Start with the letters printed in heavy type.

(*Solutions are on page 120*)

Pavel/Valeri ___Bure___

Bobby/Brett ___Hull___

Phil/Tony ___Esposito___

Kevin/Derian _____

Geoff/Russ _____

Dale/Dave _____

Eric/Brett ___Lindros___

Neal/Aaron _____

Daniel/Henrik ___Sedin___

Joe/Brian _____

Marcel/Gilbert _____

Frank/Pete _____

Max/Doug ___Weight___

Gordie/Mark ___Howe___

Scott/Rob ___Niedermyer___

Maurice/Henri ___Richard___

Brian/Brent _____

Pierre/Sylvain ___Turgeon___

Ken/Dave ___Dryden___

Wayne/Brent ___Gretzky___

Peter/Anton _____

Chris/Sean <u>Pronger</u>

66

N											E
B	I	E	D	**M**	T	A	**H**	O	P	S	**B**
E	**T**	Y	A	E	C	H	S	**B**	R	**H**	U
N	U	E	H	R	**H**	I	E	O	U	O	R
T	L	R	O	M	O	E	T	R	L	E	T
E	G	**R**	A	V	T	W	R	L	R	**D**	E
O	I	Y	R—**P**	L	T	E	Y	L	Y	N
N	E	C	O	**S**	U	I	R	D	L	**D**	K
R	**S**	N	H	N	D	E	C	E	A	I	Z
L	T	I	A	R	G	L	N	H	N	O	T
I	A	D	E	**S**	E	N	L	R	T	N	E
N	S	T	S	**H**	U	O	U	U	**M**	N	R
D	R	O	N	Y	**C**	N	T	E	R	E	**G**

6
GRETZKY GOLD

On February 24, 2002, exactly 50 years to the day after the Edmonton Mercurys won Canada's last Olympic gold medal, another Canadian team faced-off for gold against a powerful American team marking its own anniversary, 22 years and two days removed from its historic "Miracle on Ice" victory in 1980. Led by team executive-director Wayne Gretzky, Canada celebrated what proved to be a truly golden anniversary. In this chapter we celebrate the hockey heroics of the 2002 Winter Games.

(Answers are on page 73)

6.1 Before the Olympics began, ice maker Trent Evans buried what object for good luck under the ice at Salt Lake City's E Center?
A. A silver horseshoe
B. A rabbit's foot
C. A miniature Stanley Cup
D. A Canadian dollar coin

6.2 Which team at the 2002 Olympics featured a forechecking system called the "Torpedo"?
A. Canada
B. Sweden
C. Belarus
D. Finland

6.3 Prior to the medal rounds, Swedish television commentators stated that Mario Lemieux was skating like what?
A. A rocket
B. A chicken
C. An old tractor
D. His former self

6.4 Prior to its gold-medal loss to Canada in 2002, when was the last time an American men's hockey team lost on home soil at the Olympics?
A. 1932
B. 1960
C. 1980
D. 2002

6.5 How many players among the top-ranked Olympic teams—Russia, Finland, Sweden, Czech Republic, Canada and USA—were not NHLers in 2001–02?
A. Six players
B. 12 players
C. 18 players
D. 24 players

6.6 What hockey team at the 2002 Olympics had the most success with the fewest NHLers on its roster?
A. Belarus
B. Switzerland
C. Sweden
D. Finland

6.7 Who is Stacey Livingston?
A. A player
B. A trainer
C. A referee
D. A Zamboni driver

6.8 What piece of goalie equipment did Canadian netminder Martin Brodeur decorate to honour his father Denis's bronze-medal win in hockey at the 1956 Olympics?

A. His mask

B. His leg pads

C. His stick

D. His sweater

6.9 Which Olympic hockey team had the largest combined payroll based on its NHL salaries in 2001–02?

A. USA

B. Russia

C. Czech Republic

D. Canada

6.10 Which NHLer was the lowest-paid player on the Canadian and American teams at the 2002 Olympics?

A. Canada's Eric Brewer of the Edmonton Oilers

B. USA's Mike York of the New York Rangers

C. Canada's Simon Gagné of the Philadelphia Flyers

D. USA's Tom Poti of the Edmonton Oilers

6.11 Where did Team Canada executive-director Wayne Gretzky sit during Canada's warm-up skate before each game at the 2002 Olympics?

A. High in the stands

B. In the Canadian press box

C. On the players' bench

D. In the team's dressing room

6.12 Because of the 2002 Winter Games in Salt Lake City, how many games did the hometown AHL Utah Grizzlies play on the road during the Olympics?

A. 11 road games

B. 13 road games

C. 15 road games

D. 17 road games

6.13 How many players on Canada's 23-man roster played for Canadian-based NHL teams in 2001–02?

A. Two players

B. Five players

C. Eight players

D. 11 players

6.14 How many players on USA's 2002 Olympic team were born in Canada?

A. None

B. Only one player, Brett Hull

C. Two players

D. Three players

6.15 Who is Vladimir Kopat?

A. A player

B. A trainer

C. A referee

D. A Zamboni driver

6.16 What country has the most indoor rinks?

A. USA

B. Finland

C. Canada

D. Russia

6.17 Who was the leading scorer at the 2002 Olympics?

A. USA's Brett Hull

B. Sweden's Mats Sundin

C. Canada's Joe Sakic

D. USA's John LeClair

6.18 How many people in Canada watched the USA–Canada gold-medal game on television? (Prime-time TV shows that draw a million viewers are considered respectable numbers in Canada.)
A. Two million viewers
B. Four million viewers
C. Six million viewers
D. More than eight million viewers

6.19 What is the most number of Winter Olympics played by an NHLer?
A. Two Olympics
B. Four Olympics
C. Six Olympics
D. Eight Olympics

6.20 During the 2002 Winter Olympics, who was American goalie Mike Richter speaking of when he confessed: "He's sneaky... It was a beautiful play"?
A. Joe Sakic
B. Jaromir Jagr
C. Mario Lemieux
D. Mike Modano

6.21 Which 2002 Olympic team among the top six—Russia, Finland, Sweden, Czech Republic, Canada and USA— outscored the opposition by the widest margin during the tournament?
A. Canada
B. Russia
C. USA
D. Sweden

6.22 After winning Olympic gold in 2002, which three players from Canada joined the so-called "Triple-Gold Club," hockey's international grand slam of a Stanley Cup, a world championship and an Olympic gold medal?

A. Joe Sakic, Rob Blake and Brendan Shanahan

B. Rob Blake, Brendan Shanahan and Mario Lemieux

C. Brendan Shanahan, Mario Lemieux and Theo Fleury

D. Mario Lemieux, Theo Fleury and Steve Yzerman

GRETZKY GOLD
Answers

6.1 **D. A Canadian dollar coin**

The man tending the ice at the E Center, Trent Evans of Edmonton, played his part in Canada's two Olympic gold medals in hockey. Evans not only made fast, smooth ice for the speedy Canadian men's and women's teams but he secretly planted a good luck piece—a Canadian $1 loonie coin—under the ice at the centre face-off circle. Evans realized that the rink had no centre dot to indicate where the officials should drop the puck. So he iced the lucky loonie to mark the spot and obscured it with a drop of yellow paint. Both Canadian teams were told but sworn to secrecy. When Canada's women's team won gold against the Americans the gambit was almost discovered. Several Canuck players kissed and touched the ice covering the coin. Fortunately, "…the girls did a good job of keeping it secret," said Evans. After 20 days, 11 games and two gold medals, it was Wayne Gretzky, executive-director of Canada's men's team, who, at a post-Olympic press conference, pulled the coin from his jacket and revealed to the world Canada's hidden talisman, saying simply it was "for luck." "We took it out of the ice tonight and we're going to present it to the Hall of Fame. We got two gold medals out of it. That's pretty special," said Gretzky. Beneath the loonie Evans also buried a Canadian dime, which he planned to keep as a souvenir.

6.2 B. Sweden

Made famous by the Djurgardens club team in Sweden, the "Torpedo" is an aggressive forechecking system that sends four-player units into the offensive zone (three forwards deep and an offensive defenseman in the middle) to take pucks away from opponents. The fifth player, a defensive defenseman plays back to protect against odd-man rushes. "They take the boards away on the offensive side, they overload on the puck side and are really aggressive," said Canada's assistant coach Jacques Martin. The "Torpedo" is a variation of the system used by the Boston Bruins in the 1970s when, on the smaller ice surface of Boston Garden, the Bruins would pile into the other team's end and slam opponents against the boards to cough up the puck.

6.3 C. An old tractor

After Sweden handed Canada a humbling 5–2 defeat in their first Olympic meeting, Swedish TV announcers likened Canadian captain Mario Lemieux to "an old tractor." Later, the Swedish media skewered its own athletes after a costly loss to Belarus. The "old tractor," still smarting from early-season hip surgery, regained his magnificent former self as the tournament progressed and scored six points in five games.

6.4 A. 1932

On American ice USA teams are virtually unbeatable. Before their 5–2 loss to Canada on February 24, 2002, the Americans went undefeated at home with an amazing 21–0–4 record dating back to 1932. Their 70-year reign began at Lake Placid in 1932 after they lost a 2–1 overtime decision to Canada on February 4. They came back in the tournament and earned a 4–1–1 record and the silver medal. At the 1960 Winter Games in Squaw Valley, the American team won its gold medal in hockey with a perfect 7–0–0. It repeated in 1980 at Lake Placid with 6–0–1 and its famous "Miracle on Ice" gold-medal performance. In 2002, USA went 4–0–1 before its 5–2 gold-medal loss to Canada.

6.5 B. 12 players
Among the 138 players chosen to represent Russia, Finland, Sweden, Czech Republic, Canada and USA at the 2002 Olympics, only 12 players were not playing in the NHL in 2001–02. Of those 12, only six—Petr Cajanek (Czech Republic), Yegor Pedomatsky (Russia), Ilya Bryzgalov (Russia), Mattias Johansson (Sweden), Henrik Zetterberg (Sweden) and Mikael Tellqvist (Sweden)—had no NHL experience. (And of those six, three were backup goalies who never saw action at the 2002 Olympics.) Which Olympian had the most NHL experience? USA's Phil Housley with 1,408 regular-season games. Russia's Igor Larionov at 40 years, two months, was the oldest player at the world hockey tournament.

6.6 A. Belarus
Belarus, a former republic of the Soviet Union, became hockey's greatest overachievers at the 2002 Winter Games, first surviving the preliminary round and then defeating Sweden 4–3 on a fluke goal to qualify against powerhouse Canada and Russia. Its fourth-place finish exemplifies the drama of the Olympic dream, where, in one moment, one chance goal can make the impossible possible. For Belarus, a B-pool team with only one NHLer, Ruslan Salei, on its roster, that stroke of luck meant the medal round. And, in the process, the team embarrassed the mighty Swedes in one of the most lopsided match-ups of men's hockey. Compared to Belarus, Sweden suited up 21 players with NHL experience.

6.7 C. A referee
Notorious for their bias, figure-skating judges have nothing on Stacey Livingston, the American referee who officiated the women's gold-medal game between Canada and USA at the 2002 Olympics. Before a worldwide viewing audience, Livingston shamelessly out-corrupted even the most corrupt panel of figure-skating judges with her blatant favouritism, awarding USA 11 power plays—including eight in a row—compared to

just five for Canada. During the pre-Olympic tour, USA posted eight consecutive wins against Canada. But in the most important game, the Canadian women prevailed with a 3–2 nail-biter to win gold. The International Ice Hockey Federation usually uses referees from neutral countries for gold-medal games, but the only female officials rated high enough were either American or Canadian.

6.8   A. His mask

Although some goaltenders wore their own NHL masks (such as Mike Richter, who donned his New York Rangers' Lady Liberty mask), Canada's Martin Brodeur commissioned a new mask to celebrate his participation in the Olympics. Painted with red and orange streaking flames, Brodeur's mask featured a neck protector engraved with the words: "Cortina d'Ampezzo 1956" and "Salt Lake City 2002." At the 1956 Games in Cortina, Italy, Martin's father Denis won a bronze medal as goalie for Canada's Kitchener-Waterloo Dutchmen. Martin and Denis Brodeur are the only father-and-son goaltenders to win Olympic hockey medals.

6.9   D. Canada

Canada's Olympic contingent of 23 NHL players had a combined payroll of US$118,700,000, easily topping the NHL payrolls of the American (US$97,200,000), Russian (US$58,600,000) and Czech (US$50,000,000) teams. Under any other circumstances, icing Canada's No. 1 scoring line of Paul Kariya (US$10,000,000), Joe Sakic (US$9,832,727) and Mario Lemieux (US$5,200,000) would cost a team US$25,000,000. To round out the six-man squad, include defensemen Rob Blake (US$9,285,194), Chris Pronger (US$9,500,000) and goalie Martin Brodeur (US$4,705,687) and Canada suited up a starting lineup worth US$49 million. And the cost of an Olympic gold medal? Priceless.

6.10   B. USA's Mike York of the New York Rangers

Eric Brewer, Mike York, Simon Gagné and Tom Poti, all playing NHL hockey for under US$1 million in 2001–02, represent the game's future, both professionally and internationally. But York was the lowest-paid NHLer on the two national squads at US$675,000 per annum. The lowest paid Canadian was Brewer at US$907,500.

6.11 **C. On the players' bench**
After sitting high in the stands for Canada's first game, a 5–2 loss to Sweden, Wayne Gretzky "tried to change our luck" and moved to the players' bench to watch his team practice prior to the second game. As one report suggested, Gretzky might be the only general manager to take such a seat during the "meaningless warm-ups." But in the second game the Canadians beat lowly Germany, so Gretzky didn't tempt fate again, returning to the players' bench for the warm-up skate before each of the remaining four Olympic contests.

6.12 **D. 17 road games**
The 2002 Olympics forced the Utah Grizzlies out of the 10,217-seat E Center, its home rink, for a 17-game road trip from January 23 to February 24. After cleaning out their corporate offices and dressing rooms, the Grizzlies went 40 days between home games and traveled 20,041 kilometres by air and land. The AHL doesn't keep road-trip records but it's believed to be the longest road trip in AHL history. (By comparison, the Utah Jazz of the NBA played only nine road games in 25 nights.) Not the greatest of road warriors with a 7–10–1 record, the Grizzlies managed a surprising nine wins, six losses and two ties while away.

6.13 **B. Five players**
Canada iced a 100 per cent Canadian-born team but only 20 per cent of those players—Curtis Joseph (Toronto), Ed Jovanovski (Vancouver), Jarome Iginla (Calgary), Eric Brewer (Edmonton) and Ryan Smyth (Edmonton)—earned their living in 2001–02 playing for NHL clubs on Canadian soil. About 52 per cent of NHLers are Canadian.

6.14 C. Two players

USA's silver medallists at the 2002 Olympics came typically from America's hockey heartland, Michigan, Massachusetts and Minnesota; and also from less hockey-oriented regions such as Brian Leetch's home state of Texas. But two players on the 23-man squad were Canadian expatriates: Brett Hull and Adam Deadmarsh. Hull, born in Belleville, Ontario, first skated for USA at the 1986 World Championships in Moscow. Deadmarsh, from Trail, B.C., joined USA at the 1993 World Junior Championships.

6.15 A. A player

Perhaps the single most memorable play of the Olympic tournament was an 80-foot slap shot unleashed by Belarus defenseman Vladimir Kopat with two minutes left in his country's championship-round game against Sweden. Goalie Tommy Salo bungled the high shot and the puck hit his mask, bounced over his head, rolled down his back and trickled across the goal line, giving Belarus a stunning 4–3 win. Kopat, a toiler in the Russian leagues, became a national hero overnight. "I could say I saw the goalie moving out and I decided to send the puck over and behind him, but that is a joke," smiled Kopat. "I just made a shot and willed it to make a goal." After going 3–0–0 in the preliminary round, the Swedes were eliminated, an upset of staggering proportions. "When we ran out of time I couldn't believe it...I couldn't believe it was over," said Swedish forward Daniel Alfredsson. The Swedish tabloid *Expressen* published pictures of every player with his NHL salary underneath the headline: "Guilty of dishonouring their country."

6.16 C. Canada

No country makes more ice for skating and playing hockey than Canada. Its 520,700 registered players can play on 3,350 indoor rinks. (And that doesn't include countless outdoor rinks and other natural surfaces such as ponds and lakes for pick-up games.) USA supports 2,500 indoor rinks and 471,700 registered players; Finland has 202 indoor rinks and 58,800 registered players; and Russia maintains only 84 indoor rinks for its 58,400 registered players.

6.17 B. Sweden's Mats Sundin
In four games Mats Sundin scored a tournament-best nine points on five goals and four assists. Brett Hull had eight points in six games; John LeClair and Joe Sakic had seven points each in six games. LeClair led all goal scorers with six goals and Mike Modano led in assists with six.

6.18 D. More than eight million viewers
Canada's 5–2 gold-medal win against USA drew an average audience of 8.66 million people, with a peak of 10.4 million viewers tuned in for the game's final minutes. These numbers far outdistance Canada's second and third most-watched shows: Game 6 of the 1992 World Series (6.71 million) and the 1998 Academy Awards (6.6 million). NBC's telecast attracted the highest rating for a hockey broadcast since the American "Miracle on Ice" team captured gold at the 1980 Olympics. The broadcast delivered 10.7 per cent of U.S. viewers (about 11 million households)—well behind the 23.9 share who watched the 1980 Soviet Union- USA match.

6.19 C. Six Olympics
No current or former NHLer has competed in more Winter Olympics than Raimo Helminen of Finland. In fact, Helminen is just one short of the all-time record of seven Olympic starts (shared by five athletes and first achieved by bobsledder Karl-Erik Eriksson in 1984). During his Olympic career, the Finnish centre won three medals, including Finland's first ever medal in Olympic hockey, a silver at Calgary in 1988. He also won two bronzes with his Finnish teammates, in 1994 and 1998. From his first Olympics as a 19-year old rookie in Sarajevo in 1984 to his

final Winter Games in 2002 (he was chosen because fellow countryman Saku Koivu was battling non-Hodgkin's lymphoma), Helminen tallied six goals and 23 points in 35 games. Helminen played 117 NHL games (13–46–59) for the New York Rangers, Minnesota North Stars and New York Islanders between 1985 and 1989.

6.20 C. Mario Lemieux

Among the many spectacular offensive plays witnessed in men's hockey at the 2002 Olympics, one of the most memorable was an inspired Mario Lemieux move that led to Canada's first goal in the gold-medal game against USA Behind 1–0 to the Americans late in the first period, Chris Pronger appeared to feed a pass to a streaking Lemieux. But the Canadian captain let the puck go through his legs to Paul Kariya who had the open net to tie the game. Mike Richter was sensational in nets for USA. He viewed the play this way: "I can see them both there, and the pass goes practically to Mario's stick. He doesn't just not play it, he actually puts his stick there to play it, then moves his stick. It was a beautiful play, and a play you have to honour as a goalie. Obviously I honoured it a bit too much," said Richter.

6.21 C. USA

The Americans settled for a silver medal at the 2002 Olympics but proved to be the highest scoring team in the tournament, outscoring opponents 26–10. Canada recorded a 22–14 margin and Russia a 20–13 spread. Each of the three teams inflated their stats with 8–1, 7–1 and 6–4 scores against underdog Belarus.

6.22 A. Joe Sakic, Rob Blake and Brendan Shanahan

Until Salt Lake City, only 10 players in hockey history had won a Stanley Cup, a world championship and an Olympic gold medal in their careers. As hat tricks go, this threesome may just be the most elusive, considering the few opportunities NHLers once had for Olympic play. Understandably, membership to this ultra-exclusive club was all European, split between six Russians and four Swedes. But after Canada's gold medal in 2002, Sakic, Blake and Shanahan gained entry as North America's first members. For Sakic, the medal also brought some payback for earlier gloating by Colorado teammate Peter Forsberg, who scored the deciding shootout goal in Sweden's Olympic win against Canada in 1994. "At least I caught up to Peter. He did rub it in a little bit," teased Sakic. The club's original members were Tomas Jonsson, Hakan Loob and Mats Naslund, who won Olympic gold for Sweden at Lillehammer in 1994.

THE TRIPLE-GOLD CLUB

Player	World Championships	Olympic Gold	Stanley Cup
Slava Fetisov	1978/81/82/83 1986/89/90	1984/88	1997/98
Igor Larionov	1982/83/86/89	1984/88	1997/98
Tomas Jonsson	1991	1994	1989
Alexei Gusarov	1986/89/90	1988	1996
Peter Forsberg	1992/98	1994	1996/01
Alex Mogilny	1989	1988	2000
Vlad Malakov	1990	1992	2000
Hakan Loob	1987/91	1994	1989
Mats Naslund	1991	1994	1986
Val Kamensky	1986/89/90	1988	1996
Joe Sakic	1994	2002	1996/01
Rob Blake	1994/97	2002	2001
B. Shanahan	1994	2002	1997/98

Game 6

OLYMPIC METTLE

Few would argue that the most anticipated and prestigious events at the Olympic Winter Games happen at the rink. Figure skating has a certain lustre but hockey is the jewel of the Winter Games. Since 1998 when NHL players arrived on the scene in full force, the Games have taken on a new dimension with professionals mixing among amateur athletes. The NHLers below have won Olympic medals dating back to 1984. Match the players on the right and their medal ranking and year on the left. Be careful, some players such as Paul Kariya, have won medals at more than one Olympics. Each player can only be used once.

(Solutions are on page 121)

1. _____ Gold 2002/Canada	A.	Paul Kariya
2. _____ Silver 2002/USA	B.	Alexander Mogilny
3. _____ Bronze 2002/Russia	C.	Brett Hull
4. _____ Gold 1998/Czech Rep.	D.	Igor Larionov
5. _____ Silver 1998/Russia	E.	Eric Lindros
6. _____ Bronze 1998/Finland	F.	Peter Forsberg
7. _____ Gold 1994/Sweden	G.	Teemu Selanne
8. _____ Silver 1994/Canada	H.	Alexei Yashin
9. _____ Bronze 1994/Finland	I.	Dominik Hasek
10. _____ Gold 1992/Unified Team	J.	Pavel Bure
11. _____ Silver 1992/Canada	K.	Robert Lang
12. _____ Bronze 1992/Czech Rep.	L.	Nikolai Khabibulin
13. _____ Gold 1988/USSR	M.	Saku Koivu
14. _____ Gold 1984/USSR	N.	Mario Lemieux

7
TRUE OR FALSE?

The tradition of naming three stars at the end of NHL games began as a method of promoting gasoline. True or False? It's true. The venerable hockey ritual was created by Imperial Oil, the sponsor of *Hockey Night In Canada*, as a gimmick to pump up sales of its Three Stars brand of gasoline. In this chapter, we give you a 50–50 chance on these brain teasers.

(Answers are on page 86)

7.1 Wayne Gretzky earned more first and second All-Star team selections than any player in NHL history. **True or False?**

7.2 Steve Yzerman is the longest-serving captain in NHL history. **True or False?**

7.3 Patrick Roy is the only player to win the Conn Smythe Trophy as playoff MVP with two different teams. **True or False?**

7.4 Colorado's Alex Tanguay became the youngest player to score a Cup-winning goal when he beat New Jersey's Martin Brodeur in Game 6 of the 2001 finals. **True or False?**

7.5 No player holds the single-season record for penalty minutes for two different NHL franchises. **True or False?**

7.6 The only NHLer who was born in Salt Lake City did not compete in the 2002 Olympic Winter Games. **True or False?**

7.7 Ray Bourque is the only player to play for two NHL teams and have them both retire his number. **True or False?**

7.8 The Pittsburgh Penguins have produced more 50-goal scorers than any other NHL team. **True or False?**

7.9 Daniel and Henrik Sedin of the Vancouver Canucks are the first pair of twins to play together on the same NHL team. **True or False?**

7.10 Luc Robitaille is the highest-scoring left-winger in NHL history. **True or False?**

7.11 In 2001, Jaromir Jagr became the first NHL player to be traded immediately after winning a scoring title. **True or False?**

7.12 Jaromir Jagr is the only NHLer to be traded immediately after recording a 50-goal season. **True or False?**

7.13 The Tampa Bay Lightning drew the largest crowd to see an NHL game. **True or False?**

7.14 Patrick Roy is the first goalkeeper to win the Stanley Cup in three different decades. **True or False?**

7.15 No 40-year-old player has ever posted a 100-point season. **True or False?**

7.16 Wayne Gretzky did not wear No. 99 when he played his first game with the Edmonton Oilers. **True or False?**

7.17 No team has ever led the NHL in both goals scored and goals allowed in the same season. **True or False?**

7.18 Under the NHL's Collective Bargaining Agreement, the maximum allowable fine for a player is US$1,000. **True or False?**

7.19 No player has ever earned election to NHL All-Star teams as both a forward and a defenseman. **True or False?**

7.20 In 2001–02, the Detroit Red Wings became the first NHL team to ice three 500-goal scorers. **True or False?**

7.21 Vladislav Fetisov was the first Soviet player to be drafted by an NHL team. **True or False?**

7.22 No team has ever swept all four playoff series en route to winning the Stanley Cup. **True or False?**

7.23 All of the Original Six teams have met in the Stanley Cup finals on at least one occasion. **True or False?**

7.24 No player has won the Hart Trophy as league MVP in his final season. **True or False?**

7.25 Since the formation of the NHL in 1917, the Montreal Canadiens have never worn sweaters without their familiar CH crest. **True or False?**

7.26 The New York Rangers was the first New York-based team to join the NHL. **True or False?**

7.27 A player born in Venezuela won four Stanley Cups. **True or False?**

7.28 No player suited up for all of the Original Six teams. **True or False?**

7.29 No NHL goalie has ever started more than 70 consecutive games in a season. **True or False?**

7.30 The only brothers to participate in men's hockey at the 2002 Olympics were Pavel and Valeri Bure. **True or False?**

7.31 Steve Yzerman was the youngest player to skate in an NHL All-Star game. **True or False?**

TRUE OR FALSE?
Answers

7.1 False

Wayne Gretzky received 15 All-Star selections in his career, eight to the first team and seven to the second team. But that impressive total lags far behind Gordie Howe, who collected 21 All-Star berths, 12 on the first team and nine on the second team. Second to Howe is Ray Bourque with 19 All-Star selections.

7.2 True

It's been 16 years and counting since Steve Yzerman first donned the "C" for the Detroit Red Wings in 1986–87. No NHLer has ever served as a team captain for as long as Yzerman, and few players have worn the "C" with more class.

7.3 True

Five players have won the Conn Smythe Trophy more than once, but only Patrick Roy has done it with different teams. Roy bagged two Conn Smythes with Montreal in 1986 and 1993, then won the prestigious award a third time with the Colorado Avalanche in 2001.

7.4 False

Ted "Teeder" Kennedy (21 years, four months) was two months younger than Alex Tanguay (21 years, six months) when he notched the Cup-winning goal for the Toronto Maple Leafs against Montreal Canadiens netminder Bill Durnan in Game 6 of the 1947 finals.

7.5 **False**
Tie Domi and Mike Peluso both hold the single-season record for penalty minutes with two franchises. In 1993–94, Domi set the Winnipeg Jets/Phoenix Coyotes' mark with 347 minutes, and he set the Toronto Maple Leafs' standard of 365 minutes in 1997–98. Peluso set the Chicago Blackhawks' record of 408 minutes in 1991–92 and the Ottawa Senators' mark of 318 minutes in 1992–93.

7.6 **True**
Salt Lake City's Steve Konowalchuk of the Washington Capitals was one of 37 players invited to the U.S. orientation camp but the nine-year NHL veteran was forced to miss the Winter Games in his hometown after being sidelined by major reconstructive surgery on his shoulder in October 2001.

7.7 **False**
When the Colorado Avalanche retired Ray Bourque's No. 77 on November 24, 2001, he joined Gordie Howe and Bobby Hull as the only players to have their numbers retired by two different NHL teams. Bourque's No. 77 was also retired by the Boston Bruins, while Howe's No. 9 was honoured by the Detroit Red Wings and the Hartford Whalers. Hull's No. 9 was retired by the Chicago Blackhawks and the Winnipeg Jets, but unlike the other two, Hull never played any games in the NHL for Winnipeg. He spent his years with the Jets in the WHA. The most recent addition to this elite group is Wayne Gretzky, whose fabled No. 99—retired by the NHL league-wide in 1999—was also officially retired by the Edmonton Oilers and the Los Angeles Kings.

7.8 **False**
Prior to Jarome Iginla's 52-goal season with Calgary in 2001–02, Pittsburgh led all NHL teams with seven 50-goal scorers. But

Iginla's breakthrough season moved the Flames into a shared lead with the Penguins.

7.9   False

The Sedins may have attracted more publicity than any previous pair of twins, but they are not the first to play on the same NHL team. There were three previous same-team twin duos: Rich and Ron Sutter of the Philadelphia Flyers from 1983–84 to 1985–86; Patrik and Peter Sundstrom of the New Jersey Devils in 1989–90; and Peter and Chris Ferraro of the New York Rangers in 1995–96.

7.10   True

Luc Robitaille surpassed Bobby Hull's NHL record of 610 career goals by a left-winger on January 18, 2002, when he tipped a point shot past Washington Capitals goalie Olaf Kolzig to open the scoring in a 3–1 Detroit win. Ironically, Robitaille's linemate during the historic game was Brett Hull, Bobby's son. Even more eerie: Brett scored Detroit's second goal later in the opening period to tie his father's career mark of 98 game-winning goals.

7.11   True

Jaromir Jagr's brooding discontent and his huge salary demands prompted the Penguins to trade him shortly after he had won his fifth NHL scoring title in 2000–01. No other team had ever cut loose an Art Ross Trophy winner before the start of the next season, although it almost occurred in 1947–48. Six games into that campaign, the Chicago Blackhawks sent scoring champ Max Bentley to Toronto in a multi-player deal. The trade paid off for the Maple Leafs, who won the Stanley Cup that year.

7.12   False

Two NHLers besides Jaromir Jagr have been traded after 50-goal seasons. Only a couple of months after he notched 55 goals for the Los Angeles Kings in 1987–88, Jimmy Carson was sent to the Edmonton Oilers as part of the blockbuster deal that brought

Wayne Gretzky to the Kings. Carson scored 49 goals for the Oilers in 1988–89, but soon after that his career took a dive. He never again scored as many as 35 goals in a season and was out of the NHL by age 28. Pavel Bure was dealt to the Florida Panthers by the Vancouver Canucks midway through 1998–99, after scoring 50 the previous year. Bure forced the trade by refusing to report to the Canucks.

7.13 True

Believe it or not, the state of Florida set the mark for the largest attendance at an NHL game. A record crowd of 28,183 turned out to watch the Tampa Bay Lightning host the Philadelphia Flyers in Game 4 of the conference quarterfinals on April 23, 1996. The game was held at the Thunder Dome in St. Petersburg, Florida.

7.14 True

When Patrick Roy won the Cup in 2001, he entered uncharted territory. No netminder had ever won Cups in three different decades. Roy won one Cup during the 1980s (Montreal 1986), two Cups during the 1990s (Montreal 1993 and Colorado 1996) and one Cup in 2001 (Colorado).

7.15 False

The best offensive season ever registered by a 40-year-old player belongs to Gordie Howe, who racked up 103 points on 44 goals

BEST OFFENSIVE SEASONS BY +40-YEAR-OLDS

Player	Team	Season	Age	G	A	P
Gordie Howe	Detroit	1968–69	40	44	59	103
Johnny Bucyk	Boston	1975–76	40	36	47	83
Gordie Howe	Detroit	1967–68	40	39	43	82
Alex Delvecchio	Detroit	1972–73	40	18	53	71
Gordie Howe	Detroit	1969–70	42	31	40	71
Dave Keon	Hartford	1979–80	40	10	52	62

and 59 assists for the Detroit Red Wings in 1968–69. Mr. Hockey turned 41 the day after the season ended. The ageless Howe also ranks third and fifth on the list of best offensive seasons by an elder statesman.

7.16 True

When Gretzky played his first game with the WHA's Edmonton Oilers on November 3, 1978, he wore No. 20 because the Oilers did not have a jersey with his trademark double-nine. It marked the only time in his pro career that Gretzky did not wear No. 99.

7.17 False

Two teams have led the NHL in goals scored and goals allowed in the same season. In both cases, it was a Chicago club. With Dick Irvin and Babe Dye providing most of the firepower, the 1926–27 Blackhawks posted a league-high 115 goals in 44 games. But the Hawks also gave up 116 goals, the most in the league, and finished third in the American Division with a 19–22–3 record. In 1947–48, led by Doug Bentley and Roy Conacher, Chicago fired a league-best 195 goals while allowing a loop-high 225 against. The leaky defense hurt. Chicago finished in last place.

7.18 True

Considering that the average NHL salary in 2001–02 was US$1.5 million a year, or about US$18,000 a game, a US$1,000 maximum fine doesn't sound like a serious deterrent. But a suspension can jack up that total considerably, since teams aren't supposed to pay players while they are serving a suspension.

7.19 False

Two versatile old-timers—Dit Clapper of the Boston Bruins and Neil Colville of the New York Rangers—were elected to NHL All-Star teams as both forwards and defensemen. Clapper was twice voted to the second team as a right-winger (1931, 1935); three times to the first team (1939, 1940, 1941) and once to the second team (1944) as a defenseman. Colville twice made the second team at centre (1939, 1940) and once on defense (1948).

7.20 True

Considering that only 28 NHLers had recorded 500 goals at the start of the 2001–02 season, it's amazing that the Detroit Red Wings began the year with three of them in their lineup. The high-scoring trio was Brett Hull (649), Steve Yzerman (645) and Luc Robitaille (590). By mid-season, all three had joined the 600-goal club and a fourth 500-goal scorer emerged, Brendan Shanahan, setting an even higher team standard: four 500-goal scorers on one club in one season.

7.21 False

Vladislav Fetisov, chosen 201st overall at the 1978 amateur draft by Montreal, was actually the second Soviet player drafted by an NHL team. Three years before, the Philadelphia Flyers took Dynamo Riga centre Viktor Khatulev with the 160th pick overall. Khatulev never played for the Flyers.

7.22 True

Since 1987, when it became necessary to win four best-of-seven series to take the Cup, no team has swept all four playoff opponents. The 1988 Edmonton Oilers came the closest, winning 16 games and suffering only two losses.

7.23 False

As of 2001–02, the Chicago Blackhawks have never met the New York Rangers or the Boston Bruins in the Stanley Cup finals. In 10 trips to the big dance, Chicago has squared off with Montreal five times, Detroit and Toronto twice each and Pittsburgh once.

7.24 False

Talk about going out on top. In 1941–42, defenseman Tom "Cowboy" Anderson won the MVP award with the last-place

Brooklyn Americans based largely on his stellar offensive play: his 41 points ranked seventh in NHL scoring. After that season, the Americans' franchise folded and Anderson left the NHL to serve in the Canadian armed forces. He never again laced up for the big show. Cowboy concluded his career in 1947, playing for the Hollywood Wolves of the Pacific Coast Hockey League.

7.25 **False**

In 1924–25, Montreal replaced the CH crest on the front of its sweater with a red-and-white globe of the earth. The strange innovation was supposed to signify that the Canadiens were hockey's world champions, a crown they claimed for themselves after defeating the PCHA-champion Vancouver Maroons and the WCHA-champion Calgary Tigers to win the Cup in 1924.

7.26 **False**

The New York Americans were the first New York-based team to join the NHL. They came aboard in 1925–26, one year before the Rangers. The Americans were created when a famous bootlegger named Bill Dwyer bought the Hamilton Tigers and moved the franchise to Manhattan.

7.27 **True**

Rick Chartraw's four Stanley Cups is a surprise in itself, but how bizarre is it that a Cup champion hails from Caracas, Venezuela? Chartraw, who moved to the U.S. at a young age and grew up playing hockey in Erie, Pennsylvania, won his four Cups with Montreal in the 1970s.

7.28 **False**

It was long assumed that no player had suited up for all of the Original Six teams, but new research has revealed that winger Vic Lynn played one game for the New York Rangers in 1942–43. This meant that Lynn had donned the colours of all six clubs. After his one-game stint with the Rangers, Lynn began a circuit of the league, playing three games for Detroit in 1943–44; two games for Montreal in 1945–46; 213 games for Toronto from 1946–47 to 1949–50 (winning three Cups); 68 games for Boston in 1950–51 and 1951–52; and 40 games with Chicago in 1952–53 and 1953–54. As well as skating with six NHL clubs, the well-travelled Lynn also played for six American Hockey League teams, two in the Western Hockey League and one each in the Eastern Hockey League and Saskatchewan Senior Hockey League.

7.29 False

Ignoring the accepted wisdom that goalies get burnt out if you play them too much, St. Louis Blues coach Mike Keenan started goalie Grant Fuhr in a record 76 straight games in 1995–96. We'll never know how well Fuhr would have performed in the playoffs because he was sidelined by a knee injury in the second game of the opening round. The Blues were forced to use backup Jon Casey, who had played in only nine games during the season. The Blues were eliminated by Detroit in the conference semifinals.

7.30 False

The Bures were not the lone hockey-playing brothers represented at the Winter Games in Salt Lake City. Other siblings included Robert and Martin Reichel as well as Kenny and Jorgen Jonsson.

7.31 False

Although Steve Yzerman is often cited as the youngest player to play in an All-Star game, the distinction belongs to Fleming Mackell, who played in the 1947 All-Star game at the age of 18 years, five months, 13 days. In that era, the game's format called for the defending league champion to play a team of All-Stars, and Mackell, a rookie, suited up for the Cup champion Toronto Maple Leafs. Yzerman, who played in the 1984 All-Star game at the age of 18 years, eight months, 22 days old, is the youngest player to play for an NHL All-Star team.

Game 7
Odd Man Out

In each of these foursomes below, one name does not belong. See if you can spot the odd man out.

(*Solutions are on page 121*)

1. Who didn't score 70 goals in a season?
   Teemu Selanne, Steve Yzerman, Jari Kurri, Bernie Nicholls

2. Who didn't post six straight 100-point seasons?
   Guy Lafleur, Brett Hull, Peter Stastny, Bobby Orr

3. Who wasn't a No. 1 draft pick?
   Chris Pronger, Mats Sundin, Mike Modano, Joe Thornton

4. Who didn't score a Stanley Cup-winning goal?
   Mario Lemieux, Doug Gilmour, Kirk Muller, Wayne Gretzky

5. Who wasn't voted Rookie of the Year?
   Pavel Bure, Brian Leetch, Chris Drury, Patrick Roy

6. Who didn't compile 3,000 career penalty minutes?
   Dale Hunter, Chris Nilan, Dave Schultz, Marty McSorley

7. Who didn't win the Vezina Trophy?
   Grant Fuhr, Billy Smith, Tom Barrasso, Gerry Cheevers

8. Who didn't play 20 NHL seasons?
   Ron Francis, Marcel Dionne, Larry Robinson, Stan Mikita

9. Who didn't score five goals in a playoff game?
   Wayne Gretzky, Mario Lemieux, Darryl Sittler, Reggie Leach

10. Who didn't captain a Stanley Cup champion?
    Guy Carbonneau, Phil Esposito, Bob Gainey, Denis Potvin

8
BAD TO THE BONE

What is hard-nosed hockey all about? Andre "Moose" Dupont, one of the head-crackers on the hell-raising Philadelphia Flyers teams of the 1970s, may have expressed it best. Smoking a cigar in the dressing room after a road win against the Vancouver Canucks, Dupont declared: "Great game for us. We don't go to jail. We beat up their chicken forwards. We score 10 goals. We win. And," he added, tossing back a cold one, "now de Moose drinks beer."

(*Answers are on page 98*)

8.1 Who broke his team's all-time penalty-minutes record in 2001–02?
A. Rob Ray of the Buffalo Sabres
B. Tie Domi of the Toronto Maple Leafs
C. Scott Stevens of the New Jersey Devils
D. Derian Hatcher of the Dallas Stars

8.2 Which musician recorded a controversial song about hockey violence in 2001, entitled "Hit Somebody!"?
A. Tom Waits
B. Warren Zevon
C. Neil Young
D. Weird Al Yankovic

8.3 Who holds the NHL record for compiling the most penalty minutes in a season in which he scored 50 goals?
A. Keith Tkachuk
B. Brendan Shanahan
C. Kevin Stevens
D. Gary Roberts

8.4 Which NHLer punched his own goalie at the 1992 World Junior Championships?

A. Jason Arnott

B. Saku Koivu

C. Radek Bonk

D. Darius Kasparaitis

8.5 Toronto Maple Leafs tough guy Tie Domi was hit with a US$1,000 fine for doing what to a fan at a game in March 2001?

A. Swearing at him

B. Squirting water at him

C. Throwing a snowball at him

D. Hitting him with his stick

8.6 Who set an NHL record for most fighting majors by a rookie in 2000–01?

A. Reed Low of the St. Louis Blues

B. Andy Sutton of the Minnesota Wild

C. Joey Tetarenko of the Florida Panthers

D. Dale Purinton of the New York Rangers

8.7 Who has been tagged with the most suspensions of any player in NHL history?

A. Tie Domi

B. Matthew Barnaby

C. Craig Berube

D. Bryan Marchment

8.8 Which team established a new NHL record for most penalty minutes in one period during a fight-filled game in 2001–02?

A. The Calgary Flames

B. The Buffalo Sabres

C. The Chicago Blackhawks

D. The New Jersey Devils

8.9 Which Boston Bruins tough guy was involved in what TV commentator Don Cherry called the "greatest fight I've ever seen"?
A. Jay Miller
B. John Wensink
C. Stan Jonathan
D. Terry O'Reilly

8.10 How many games did the Philadelphia Flyers go unbeaten after acquiring heavyweight Donald Brashear on December 17, 2001?
A. Five Games
B. Eight games
C. 11 games
D. 14 games

8.11 Who was accused of assaulting the San Jose Sharks mascot Sharkie in 2001–02?
A. Chris Chelios of the Detroit Red Wings
B. Theo Fleury of the New York Rangers
C. Ed Belfour of the Dallas Stars
D. Darcy Tucker of the Toronto Maple Leafs

8.12 Who is the only NHLer to score 40 or more goals in a season while collecting more than 300 minutes in penalties?
A. Al Secord
B. Dave Semenko
C. Clark Gillies
D. Keith Tkachuk

8.13 What is the NHL record for the worst goals-to-penalty-minutes ratio among players with more than 1,000 career penalty minutes?
A. One goal for every 160 PIM
B. One goal for every 260 PIM
C. One goal for every 360 PIM
D. One goal for every 460 PIM

8.14 Who was the first NHLer to rack up 1,000 career penalty minutes?
   A. Eddie Shore
   B. Red Horner
   C. Ted Lindsay
   D. Lou Fontinato

8.15 Which legendary enforcer scored two goals and won a fight against the league's meanest player in his first NHL game?
   A. Ted Lindsay
   B. John Ferguson
   C. Dave Schultz
   D. Chris Nilan

8.16 What is the record for most points in a season by an NHL penalty leader?
   A. 42 points
   B. 52 points
   C. 62 points
   D. 72 points

BAD TO THE BONE
Answers

8.1   **B. Tie Domi of the Toronto Maple Leafs**
Domi surpassed Tiger Williams as Toronto's penalty king in trademark style: dispensing vigilante justice. The Maple Leafs' enforcer tossed Montreal's Reid Simpson to the ice after he had roughed up mild-mannered Leaf Anders Eriksson. George Thorogood's "Bad to the Bone" boomed out of the speakers at the Air Canada Centre as Domi took his seat in the penalty box. The minor gave him 1,672 penalty minutes in a Toronto uniform, two more than Williams. The record-setting feat did not go unrecognized by Domi's teammates, several of whom glided over

to tap him with a stick after he emerged from the sin bin. Coach Pat Quinn also congratulated Domi when he returned to the bench. As Quinn said after his club had posted a 6–4 victory, "This is a physical, brutal game sometimes and people who can play and who also have that [policeman] ability make the game a little more sane." The only thing that bothered Domi about setting the record was that no mention of it was made to the capacity crowd. "It just goes to show you that certain people don't like that part of the game," said Domi.

8.2 B. Warren Zevon

Warren Zevon, a rabid hockey fan, and Mitch Albom, a Detroit sportswriter, collaborated on "Hit Somebody!" The tongue-in-cheek tune relates the story of Buddy, from the fictional Canadian border town of Big Beaver, who dreams of scoring goals, but is really only good at beating up other players. When Buddy tries to argue he's more than your average goon, his coach replies: "The fast guys get paid, they shoot, they score. Protect them Buddy, that's what you're here for. Protection is what you're here for. Protection—it's the stars that score. Protection—kick somebody's ass." Although it earned critical acclaim, "Hit Somebody!" was not well received by the NHL, which banned the tune from the playlist at NHL arenas.

8.3 C. Kevin Stevens

Putting the POW in power forward, Stevens accumulated a team-leading 254 penalty minutes in 1991–92, while notching 54 goals for the Pittsburgh Penguins. The six-foot-three, 230-pound left-winger ranked second in league scoring that season with 123 points, only eight behind teammate Mario Lemieux.

Most Penalty Minutes by 50-Goal Scorers

Player	Team	Season	G	PIM
Kevin Stevens	Pittsburgh	1991–92	54	254
Keith Tkachuk	Phoenix	1996–97	52	228
Brendan Shanahan	St. Louis	1993–94	52	211
Gary Roberts	Calgary	1991–92	53	207
Al Secord	Chicago	1982–83	54	180
Kevin Stevens	Pittsburgh	1992–93	55	177

8.4 D. Darius Kasparaitis

Kasparaitis is known as the mad Lithuanian, with good reason. The rugged rearguard earned a spot in hockey lore by punching his own goalie in the nose at the 1992 World Junior Championships. Kasparaitis's team, the former Soviet Union, known that year as the Commonwealth of Independent States (C.I.S.), was filing off the bench to console goalie Ildar Muhametov after a 5–1 loss to the Czech Republic, when Kasparaitis struck. "I was mad because the Czech team was bad that year and they had still beat us. So, I snapped," confessed Kasparaitis in an interview with the *National Post*. "I got fined for it but it was worth it. That goalie didn't play anymore after that and Nikolai Khabibulin was the backup, and he played unbelievable the rest of the tournament." Improbably, the C.I.S. rebounded to win the gold medal, and Kasparaitis was named the tourney's outstanding defenseman.

8.5 B. Squirting water at him

When fans began tossing garbage at Tie Domi after he entered the penalty box at Philadelphia's First Union Center on March 29, 2001, Domi responded by grabbing a water bottle and spraying them. This prompted Chris Falcone, a portly 36-year-old Flyers fan, to leap out of his seat and charge the penalty box. When Falcone hit the Plexiglass it gave way, sending him tumbling into the box, where a melee ensued. After being fined US$1,000 by the NHL for his actions, Domi confessed that he "shouldn't have lowered himself to squirt water," but added, "That's our territory. Fans pay to watch the game, not get involved in the game. That's when it can get ugly."

8.6   A.   Reed Low of the St. Louis Blues
After three years of battling all comers in the minors, Low won a spot on the St. Louis Blues roster in 2000–01 by doing what he does best: answering the bell. The six-foot-four 225-pound right-winger finished the year with a team-high 159 penalty minutes and was second in the NHL with 23 fighting majors, setting a new record for rookies.

8.7   D.   Bryan Marchment
On November 9, 2001, San Jose Sharks defenseman Bryan Marchment was given a six-game suspension for knocking Carolina Hurricanes forward Shane Willis unconscious with a vicious elbow. The suspension was the 14th of Marchment's career, the most in NHL history. Marchment earned previous suspensions for head-butting, checking from behind, kneeing, spearing and uttering racist slurs. Despite the NHL's avowed mandate to clean up the game, the longest suspension that Marchment has ever received for his crimes is eight games.

8.8   A.   The Calgary Flames
The mayhem began when Calgary's Craig Berube drew charging and roughing penalties for slamming into Anaheim Mighty Ducks netminder Jean-Sebastien Giguere at 15:44 of the third period during the December 8, 2001, game. A few minutes later, Ducks enforcer Kevin Sawyer steamed into the Calgary crease and cross-checked goalie Mike Vernon in the head, sending him crashing into the net. Several fights broke out, including one in which Anaheim's Denny Lambert traded blows with Calgary scoring star Jarome Iginla. A total of 279 penalty minutes were assessed in the last 85 seconds of the game. Calgary racked up 190 penalty

minutes in the period, breaking a 23-year NHL record of 188 minutes set by the Philadelphia Flyers in March 1979.

8.9   C. Stan Jonathan

At five-foot-eight and 175 pounds, Jonathan was no heavyweight, but he hit like one. Nicknamed Bulldog because of his chunky build and tenacity, Jonathan rarely, if ever, lost a fight. During the fourth game of the 1978 finals, Jonathan tangled with Montreal's Pierre Bouchard, who stood six-foot-two and weighed 230 pounds. Bruins coach Don Cherry called it the greatest fight he'd ever seen. "Boy, does Pierre start off great. He is lifting Stan off the ice and throwing him around. I'm on the bench and I say, 'Uh-oh, Stan looks like he's bitten off more than he can chew.' All of a sudden Stan switches hands, from a righty to a lefty. This is tough for Pierre and it catches him off balance. Stan landed a heavy left and Pierre started to go down, but as he's falling Stan pours about three more on him, then the coup de grace, as they say, was just as Pierre hit the ice. The blood was everywhere, even on linesman John D'Amico."

8.10   B. Eight games

Philadelphia coach Bill Barber insisted that the Flyers had not acquired Donald Brashear in a trade with the Vancouver Canucks simply to be a fighter. Said Barber: "We got him to be a role player and to be an effective role player in this league, you need to be able to make the proper plays at the right time. Donald does that." Brashear backed up Barber's claim during a game on January 19, 2002, against Toronto in which he scored the game-winner, beating Curtis Joseph with a crackling slap shot, and also won two scraps with Tie Domi. Brashear's menacing presence seemed to give the Flyers a lift. The club embarked on a season-high eight-game winning streak after he joined the squad.

8.11   B. Theo Fleury of the New York Rangers

During a six-game midseason road trip in 2001–02, Fleury exhibited some bizarre behaviour, both on and off the ice. In a

January 5 game against Pittsburgh, the Rangers hothead picked up three slashing minors. After the last one, he left the ice and went to the dressing room with 7:37 remaining and his team trailing 3–1. He didn't return. By the time the game ended, Fleury was already on the team bus. Earlier in the same road trip, he was ejected from a game in San Jose after he received a kneeing major for a deliberate attempt to injure. En route to the dressing room, Fleury reportedly punched San Jose's costumed mascot, Sharkie, who suffered a rib injury. Fleury denied the attack, but seemed unrepentant about his emotional outbursts, telling reporters: "So I've had a few cases of snap-itis. That's nothing new. I had plenty of snap-itis attacks in Calgary didn't I?"

8.12 A. Al Secord
It's doubtful that the Boston Bruins would have traded Secord if Don Cherry had not been fired prior to the 1980–81 season. Secord fit Cherry's definition of an ideal Bruin: big, tough, with a deft touch around the net. But on December 18, 1980, general manager Harry Sinden sent the burly left-winger to Chicago in exchange for defenseman Mike O'Connell. Playing on Chicago's top line with Denis Savard and Steve Larmer, Secord developed into one of the league's premier power forwards. In 1981–82, he scored 44 goals and racked up 303 penalty minutes. No other 300-PIM man has ever scored as many goals.

8.13 C. One goal for every 360 PIM
Randy Holt played 10 NHL seasons and 395 regular-season games despite scoring just four goals. Clearly, he wasn't kept around because of his offensive skills. Holt, who shuttled between defense and the wing, earned a big-league paycheque because he wasn't shy about dropping his gloves. Included among his career total of 1,438 penalty minutes is the record-setting 67 penalty minutes he compiled in one game against the Philadelphia Flyers on March 11, 1979. Holt, who was with the Los Angeles Kings at the time, picked up one minor, three majors, two 10-minute

misconducts and three game misconducts. Quite a night's work. Holt's ratio of one goal for every 360 penalty minutes is an NHL high for players with 1,000 penalty minutes or more.

8.14 B. Red Horner

The Toronto Maple Leafs' hardrock led the league in penalty minutes a record eight straight seasons from 1932–33 to 1939–40. Horner became the first NHLer to reach 1,000 penalty minutes in 1936–37. Two years later, Eddie Shore became the second player to crack the milestone.

8.15 B. John Ferguson

Montreal Canadiens coach Toe Blake gave Ferguson specific instructions prior to his first NHL game against the Boston Bruins on October 8, 1963. "You'll be playing on a line with Béliveau and Geoffrion tonight. Don't let those Boston buggers bother my big scorers or push them around." Blake undoubtedly had Bruins defenseman "Terrible" Teddy Green in mind. Ferguson didn't wait long to introduce himself to the Bruins' resident psycho. Just 12 seconds into the game the two collided and the gloves flew off. Ferguson sent a message by thumping out a resounding decision. But the hard-nosed rookie wasn't done. He later scored two goals and then set up the game-tying marker by Bernie Geoffrion in a 4–4 deadlock. With Ferguson handling policing duties, Montreal would capture five Cups in the next eight years.

8.16 C. 62 points

Players who spend a lot of time in the penalty box don't usually bag many points, but Bob Probert and Dave "Tiger" Williams both managed to compile a respectable 62 points during a season in which they also led the NHL in penalty minutes. In 1987–88, Probert notched 29 goals and 33 assists for the Detroit Red Wings, while racking up 398 penalty minutes. Both marks were career highs. Williams posted 35 goals and 27 assists for the Vancouver Canucks to go with 343 penalty minutes in 1980–81.

Game 8

MVP MAVERICK

With one exception, a Canadian has been named playoff MVP every year since 1964, when the Conn Smythe Trophy was first awarded. To find that exceptional player, unscramble the names below on the left by placing each letter in the correct order in the boxes on the right. To help, each name starts with the bolded letter. Next, unscramble the letters in the circled boxes to spell the first name of our secret MVP; then the diamond-shaped boxes for his last name; and square-shaped boxes for his team.

(Solutions are on page 121)

YOR

VESNETS

SNOOBRIN

THAXELL

YANGEI

SIACK

NYDDER

of the

9
STANLEY IS IN THE BUILDING

Ray Bourque's final NHL goal was an historic one. When the 40-year-old defenseman blasted a shot past New Jersey Devils goalie Martin Brodeur in the third period of Game 3 of the 2001 Stanley Cup finals, he became the oldest player to score in the finals. Bourque went out a winner in his last season. Let's see how you fare in our concluding chapter.

(*Answers are on page 111*)

9.1 What slogan did Colorado's Ray Bourque have written on his baseball cap during the 2001 playoffs?
  A. Chase The Dream
  B. True Believer
  C. Mission 16W
  D. The Last Dance

9.2 Which Stanley Cup champion of the 1990s featured a record six players who were former captains of other NHL clubs?
  A. The 1992 Pittsburgh Penguins
  B. The 1994 New York Rangers
  C. The 1997 Detroit Red Wings
  D. The 1999 Dallas Stars

9.3 In which playoff game does Wayne Gretzky believe he turned in his finest NHL performance?
  A. Game 5 of the 1984 finals against the New York Islanders
  B. Game 3 of the 1985 finals against Philadelphia
  C. Game 2 of the 1988 semifinals against Calgary
  D. Game 7 of the 1993 semifinals against Toronto

9.4 Reggie Leach equalled an NHL record by scoring five goals for the Philadelphia Flyers in a game during the 1976 playoffs. What made Leach's effort doubly impressive?
  A. He had an injured wrist
  B. He had not slept the night before
  C. He was wearing someone else's skates
  D. He was drunk

9.5 Which Colorado player celebrated his team's Stanley Cup triumph in 2001 by wearing his hockey equipment for 25 hours?
  A. Dan Hinote
  B. Milan Hejduk
  C. Shjon Podein
  D. Chris Dingman

9.6 How much money did each member of the Colorado Avalanche earn for winning the Stanley Cup in 2001?
  A. US$70,000
  B. US$140,000
  C. US$280,000
  D. US$350,000

9.7 Who has played in the most playoff games in NHL history?
  A. Mark Messier
  B. Guy Carbonneau
  C. Patrick Roy
  D. Claude Lemieux

9.8 Which Stanley Cup finals featured a bizarre game in which play was delayed several times by heavy fog?
  A. The 1948 Toronto-Detroit finals
  B. The 1965 Montreal-Chicago finals
  C. The 1970 Boston-St. Louis finals
  D. The 1975 Philadelphia-Buffalo finals

9.9 "Mighty Mouse" was the nickname of which 1954 Detroit Red Wings playoff hero?

A. Alex Delvecchio

B. Tony Leswick

C. Johnny Wilson

D. Marty Pavelich

9.10 In 2001, Patrick Roy came within one minute and 41 seconds of breaking the mark for the longest span of shutout goaltending in the Cup finals. Which New Jersey player broke Roy's streak?

A. Bob Corkum

B. John Madden

C. Patrik Elias

D. Sergei Brylin

9.11 How much time does each player on the Stanley Cup-winning team get to spend with the Cup during the summer?

A. Six hours

B. One day

C. Three days

D. Six days

9.12 Where did Colorado coach Bob Hartley take the Stanley Cup to celebrate the Avalanche's championship in 2001?

A. To a factory

B. To a race track

C. To a hospital

D. To a golf course

9.13 As of 2001, there have been 28 recipients of the Jack Adams Award as coach of the year. How many of those 28 winners won the trophy in the same year that they coached a Stanley Cup champion?

A. Two coaches
B. Six coaches
C. 10 coaches
D. 14 coaches

9.14 In 2001, the *Hockey News* assembled a panel to pick the players they felt would have won the Conn Smythe Trophy as playoff MVP in the years before the award existed (1918 to 1964). Who would have won the most Conn Smythes?

A. Gordie Howe
B. Maurice Richard
C. Turk Broda
D. Howie Morenz

9.15 Which club set an unwanted record in the 2000 playoffs, when it recorded an all-time NHL low of six shots in a game?

A. The Edmonton Oilers
B. The Toronto Maple Leafs
C. The Florida Panthers
D. The Ottawa Senators

9.16 The final game of which series drew the largest Canadian TV audience ever to watch a playoff broadcast?

A. The 1967 finals between Toronto and Montreal
B. The 1987 finals between Edmonton and Philadelphia
C. The 1993 semifinals between Toronto and Los Angeles
D. The 1994 finals between Vancouver and New York

9.17 Who is the only goalie to surrender two Stanley Cup-winning goals in overtime during his career?

A. Turk Broda

B. Gerry McNeil

C. Andy Moog

D. Pete Peeters

9.18 Teams from how many different Canadian cities have won the Stanley Cup?

A. Six cities

B. Eight cities

C. 10 cities

D. 12 cities

9.19 Which playoff upset is known as the "Miracle on Manchester"?

A. Chicago's upset of Toronto in the 1938 finals

B. Toronto's upset of Detroit in the 1949 finals

C. Los Angeles's upset of Edmonton in the 1982 division semifinals

D. The Islanders' upset of Pittsburgh in the 1993 division finals

9.20 Six father-and-son combinations have played for Stanley Cup champions. How many of those combos won the Cup with the same franchise?

A. None

B. One

C. Two

D. Three

STANLEY IS IN THE BUILDING
Answers

9.1   **C. Mission 16W**

The most emotional moment of the 2001 postseason occurred when Colorado Avalanche captain Joe Sakic accepted the Stanley Cup from NHL commissioner Gary Bettman and handed the silverware to Ray Bourque. The 40-year-old defenseman had trouble holding back the tears. After 22 years, he had finally won hockey's ultimate prize. Throughout the playoffs, Bourque's teammates tried to downplay the media's persistent questions about winning the Cup for the future Hall of Famer, but when the mission was finally accomplished, they admitted it had a been a rallying cry. "I talked to Ray before the year started and told him that we were going to win and that I wanted him to be the first one to lift it," said Sakic. "That was the goal from day one." Bourque called his championship chase Mission 16W—16 play-off wins to get the Cup—and had caps bearing the slogan made up to hand out in the dressing room.

9.2   **D. The 1999 Dallas Stars**

The Stars' 1999 roster was laden with veteran leaders. In addition to captain Derian Hatcher, six other Dallas players had previously captained NHL teams. The list included Guy Carbonneau (Montreal, 1989–94), Mike Keane (Montreal, 1994–96), Joe Nieuwendyk (Calgary, 1991–95), Brett Hull (St. Louis, 1992–96), Pat Verbeek (Hartford, 1992–95) and Brian Skrudland (Florida, 1993–97).

9.3   **D. Game 7 of the 1993 semifinals against Toronto**

Although it's hard to imagine that by 1993 Wayne Gretzky still felt he had things to prove, the Great One would later admit that he was highly motivated to turn in a stellar effort against the Toronto Maple Leafs on May 29, 1993. Gretzky had been criticized for his play earlier in the series when his team, the Los Angeles Kings, fell behind three games to two. He was especially stung by the comments of *Toronto Sun* columnist Bob McKenzie, who said that Gretzky looked like he was "skating with a piano on his back." No. 99 scored the overtime winner in Game 6 to send the series back to Toronto, then on the morning of the deciding game, he told his father, "This is one piano that has another tune to play." That night, Gretzky scored three goals and two assists to carry the Kings to a 5–4 victory and earn a trip to his last Cup finals. After retiring, he identified it as "the best NHL game I ever played."

9.4 D. He was drunk
On May 6, 1976, Philadelphia Flyers winger Reggie Leach scored five goals in a 6–3 win over the Boston Bruins in Game 5 of the semifinals. The stunning performance was even more remarkable considering that Leach was, by his own admission, "stone drunk." As described in the book *When The Final Buzzer Sounds,* Leach had gotten hammered the night before and only made the rink that afternoon thanks to two teammates, who went to his house and revived him from a drunken stupor with a cold shower and a quart of coffee. After this treatment, Leach decided that his best chance of making it through the 1:00 pm Sunday matinee was to have a few more drinks. With a few fresh beers in his system, he arrived at the Spectrum feeling "really loose." Leach told linemate Bobby Clarke, "Just get me the puck. I'll put it in." Two hours later, the Flyers had posted a 6–3 victory, Leach had matched the record for most goals in a playoff game and the Bruins were gone from the playoffs.

9.5 C. Shjon Podein
Podein was still seated in the dressing room after his teammates had left for a restaurant to celebrate their Stanley Cup win, when one of the player's wives suggested that he wear his uniform to the party. Podein did just that, donning skate guards to soften his

steps on the dance floor. At the party, former NHL coach Barry Melrose told Podein that he'd once seen another player wear his uniform for 24 hours in Adirondack. As the Avalanche winger later confessed, "That was the triple-dog dare right there. I had to do it." After the party, Podein and his wife went home to bed, where he slept in his gear with the family dog between them. "My dog didn't mind the smell, but my wife thought it was disgusting," said Podein, who met friends later that day for lunch outside Denver, then went to a tavern still wearing his sweaty duds. The stunt ended 25 hours after it began with Podein jumping into a creek at sunset. "My feet were pretty sore from wearing the skates," he conceded. "It was 20 per cent funny and 80 per cent dumb. It's something I'll always remember, though."

9.6 **A. US$70,000**
When they say that players compete for the "love of the Cup," they're not exaggerating. NHLers make far less money during the playoffs than in the regular season. Instead of being paid by their individual teams, players receive a cut from the playoff awards pool, the size of which depends on how far their team advances. As reward for surviving 23 hard-fought postseason games, each player on the 2001 champion Colorado Avalanche received about US$70,000. In comparison, for playing 23 games during the regular season, the average NHLer in 2000–01 earned US$1.4 million, while superstars made much more. The rewards for players on losing playoff teams is even less. Each member of the Cup finalist New Jersey Devils took home about US$50,000 each, while players on teams that were eliminated in the first round made just US$9,000 a piece.

9.7 **C. Patrick Roy**
Roy added to his growing hoard of playoff records when he played his 237th postseason game against the Detroit Red Wings on May 25, 2002, surpassing Mark Messier as the all-time leader in the category. The Colorado netminder's sustained level of

excellence and longevity are remarkable. The closest goalie to Roy in playoff games is Grant Fuhr with 150.

9.8 **D. The 1975 Philadelphia-Buffalo finals**
Stifling heat and oppressive humidity in Buffalo's Memorial Auditorium created an eerie, low-lying fog in Game 3 of the 1975 finals. Surveying the thick soup, Philadelphia Flyers goalie Bernie Parent cracked, "I wouldn't take my boat out in these conditions." Play had to be halted 12 times during the game because visibility was so poor. Officials finally resorted to having rink attendants skate around waving blankets to disperse the mist. In the end, the fog worked to the Sabres' advantage. Rene Robert scored the winner in overtime, beating Parent on a shot from a nearly impossible angle. "It went between his pads and the post," said Robert. "It was pure luck. Any other time I wouldn't have shot the puck, but because of the fog you could score from anywhere."

9.9 **B. Tony Leswick**
Tony Leswick, who died of cancer at age 79 in July 2001, is best remembered as the scoring hero of the 1954 Stanley Cup finals. The diminutive but feisty winger, who was nicknamed "Mighty Mouse," stood five-foot-six and weighed 160 pounds. Although he usually played a checking role with the Red Wings, Leswick's most lasting claim to fame came on April 16, 1954, when he scored the winning goal against Montreal in the seventh game in overtime. Leswick's Cup-clincher was no work of art. Near the end of his first shift in the extra period, he flipped the puck into the Canadiens' zone, then watched in amazement as it deflected off defenseman Doug Harvey's arm and past goalie Gerry McNeil.

9.10 **A. Bob Corkum**
Patrick Roy entered Game 2 of the 2001 Stanley Cup finals against New Jersey riding a streak of 213 minutes, 12 seconds of shutout hockey in the finals. He hadn't been scored on since Game 3 of the 1996 finals. Roy needed to blank the Devils for

16 minutes, 11 seconds to snap the all-time mark of 229:22, set by Clint Benedict between 1923 and 1926. But Roy's run at the record came up 1:41 short, when he was beaten through the five-hole by Bob Corkum, who had just helped kill off a Devils' penalty. Corkum was a surprise starter, having been added to the lineup to replace injured winger Randy McKay.

9.11 B. One day
The custom of each player on a championship team getting to spend 24 hours with the Stanley Cup is a recent innovation. It began in 1995 when the New Jersey Devils won the Cup for the first time. Hockey Hall of Fame curator Phil Pritchard and three of his colleagues take turns accompanying the trophy on its travels. Players have brought the Cup up on mountain tops, to strip clubs and even gravesites. One of the stranger trips occurred in 1999, when Jere Lehtinen of the Dallas Stars had the Finnish army take the Cup on a hovercraft to an island in the Baltic Sea where he had a sauna party with all his childhood buddies.

9.12 A. To a factory
Before Bob Hartley became a full-time coach, he worked for four years at the PPG windshield plant in his hometown of Hawkesbury, Ontario. Hartley had promised his friends at the factory that if he ever won the Stanley Cup he'd bring it to the plant. On July 31, 2001, he kept that promise. Hartley's day began with a 6 a.m. fishing expedition on the Ottawa River, then continued to the PPG factory with North America's most recognizable trophy in tow. There were 1,200 people waiting when he showed up.

9.13 A. Two coaches
The voters don't like giving the Jack Adams Award to coaches who win championships. Only twice in 28 years has the trophy gone to a bench boss who captured the Cup. The two who managed the rare double were the award's inaugural winner, Fred Shero of the Philadelphia Flyers in 1974 and Scotty Bowman of

the Montreal Canadiens in 1977. Glen Sather, who coached the Edmonton Oilers to four Cups in five years, won the award in 1986, the one year in that string that Edmonton was knocked out of the playoffs. Al Arbour, who piloted the New York Islanders to four straight Cups from 1980 to 1984, won the Adams in 1979, a year in which the Isles were ousted in the quarterfinals.

9.14 B. Maurice Richard
According to the *Hockey News'* panel, the complete list of multiple Conn Smythe Trophy winners would include four new names: Jack Darragh (1920, 1921), Ted Kennedy (1947, 1948), Gordie Howe (1955, 1964) and Maurice "Rocket" Richard, who would have claimed the trophy three times (1951, 1953, 1958). The Montreal right-winger might also have won it a fourth time in 1944, a year in which the panel picked Richard's linemate, Toe Blake. The numbers suggest it was a toss-up: Blake posted 18 points on seven goals and 11 assists, while Richard counted 17 points on 12 goals and five assists. Hockey fans are aware that the Rocket was a tremendous player, but seeing his name attached to three or four Conn Smythes would be added evidence of his postseason panache.

9.15 B. The Toronto Maple Leafs
Like a doomed rat in the suffocating grasp of a python, the Leafs quietly expired 3–0 to the New Jersey Devils in Game 6 of their 2000 semifinals series. Facing elimination, Toronto managed only three quality scoring chances in the entire game and missed the net on each one, allowing Martin Brodeur to breeze to the easiest shutout of his career. The Leafs directed a paltry six shots on net: three in the first period, two in the second and one in the third. That's the fewest shots recorded in an NHL game since the stat was first compiled in 1967–68. The previous record-holder was the Washington Capitals, who had seven shots on net in a 4–1 loss to Philadelphia on February 12, 1978.

9.16 D. The 1994 finals between Vancouver and New York

Early in the 1994 finals it appeared that the New York Rangers might blow the Vancouver Canucks away, but after the Blueshirts went up three games to one, the tide turned. The resurgent Canucks roared back to take the next two games, 6–3 and 4–1, and send the series back to Manhattan for Game 7. The dramatic finale, won 3–2 by the Rangers, drew a record TV audience of 4.96 million, exceeding the 4.27 million that watched the last game of the 1993 semifinal between Toronto and Los Angeles.

9.17 B. Gerry McNeil

Although McNeil posted a superb 1.89 goals-against average in 35 playoff games, the Montreal Canadiens netminder bears the stigma of being the only goalie to give up two Stanley Cup-winning overtime goals in his career. The first occurred in Game 5 of the 1951 series, when Toronto's Bill Barilko fired the winner past McNeil at 2:53 of the first overtime period. In the 1954 finals, McNeil and his Montreal mates went down to defeat when Detroit's Tony Leswick scored the Cup-clincher at 4:29 of the first overtime stanza.

9.18 C. 10 cities

In 75 years of NHL playoff hockey only four Canadian teams have won the Stanley Cup: Montreal, Toronto, Edmonton and Calgary. However, in hockey's early days a number of Canadian hamlets claimed the silver chalice. The six other Canadian Cup-winning cities are Ottawa, Kenora, Quebec City, Winnipeg, Vancouver and Victoria.

9.19 C. Los Angeles's upset of Edmonton in the 1982 division semifinals

In 1981–82, the Edmonton Oilers emerged as a powerhouse, finishing second to the New York Islanders in the overall standings and claiming their first Smythe Division flag. Led by Wayne Gretzky, who rewrote the record book with a 92-goal, 212-point season, Edmonton became the first team in history to reach the 400-goal mark. But all that gaudy offense went to waste in the playoffs, as the Oilers were ambushed by the fourth-place Los Angeles Kings in the best-of-five division semifinals. The turning point came in Game 3 when the Kings rallied from a 5–0 deficit, forcing overtime on a goal by Steve Bozek at 19:55, then winning the game on a goal by rookie Daryl Evans at 2:25 of sudden death. The comeback became known as the "Miracle on Manchester," after the location of the Kings' arena on Manchester Boulevard in Inglewood, California.

9.20 **C. Two**
Only two father-and-son tandems have won the Cup as players for the same franchise. The first duo was Lester and Lynn Patrick and it was entirely due to freak circumstance. Lester was the coach of the New York Rangers Cup-winning team in 1928, but when netminder Lorne Chabot was injured in Game 2 of the finals, he went into the net as an emergency replacement and won the game in overtime. In 1940, Lester's son Lynn got his name on the Cup with the Rangers. The only other father-and-son combo to win the Cup with the same team was Butch and Pierre Bouchard. Butch bagged Cups with the Montreal Canadiens in 1944, 1946, 1953 and 1956, while Pierre claimed the prize with Montreal in 1971, 1973, 1976, 1977 and 1978.

SOLUTIONS TO GAMES

Game 1: Hockey Crossword

Y	Z	E	R	M	A	N	S	H	A	N	A	H	A	N
U	L		E	E	U		I	O		A				
S	T	I	L	L	M	A	N	L	I	N	D	R	O	S
H	A		L	L	L		E		T					H
K	A	S	P	A	R	A	I	T	I	S	B	O	N	K
E	F		N	A		O		Y		N				A
V	A	L	K	B	A	L	O	N	O	L	I	V	E	R
I	E		Y		T		E	K		E				I
C	L	U	T	C	H	O	I	L	E	R	S	R	O	Y
H	R		H	W		L		U		B				A
R	A	Y	N	E	R	E	L	I	K	P	R	E	S	S
O	A		L		A		G		P		E			A
V	A	N	B	I	E	S	B	R	O	U	C	K	O	T
E	D		O		E		A		W		E			A
R	A	Y	A	S	T	L	E	Y	R	E	D	D	E	N

Game 2: Frère Jacques (French 101)

1. E. Patrick Roy, King
2. J. Pat LaFontaine, The Fountain
3. L. Simon Gagné, Win
4. G. Eric Desjardins, The Gardens
5. B. Michel Petit, Small
6. A. Guy Lafleur, The Flower
7. D. Jacques Lemaire, The Major
8. C. Vincent Lecavalier, The Rider
9. K. Wilf Paiement, Payment
10. H. Sylvain Côté, Side
11. I. Rod Brind'Amour, Little Bit of Love
12. F. Mario Lemieux, The Best

Game 3: The First Five-Team 20-Goal Man

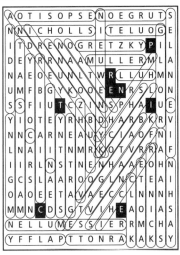

The first NHLer with 20 goals on five teams is Dean PRENTICE, who scored at least 20 goals with each team he played on—New York Rangers, Boston, Detroit, Pittsburgh and Minnesota—between 1952–53 and 1973–74.

Game 4: *Not*-Wayne-Gretzky-Offensive Records

1. Old-timer Joe Malone scored a league-record seven goals on January 31, 1920, two better than Wayne Gretzky, who notched five-goal games on four occasions.

2. Tim Kerr scored 34 power-play goals in 1985–86. Gretzky's best season was 1982–83 when he recorded 20 man-advantage goals.

3. Mario Lemieux scored a league-high 13 shorthanded goals in 1988–89 followed by Gretzky's 12 shorthanded goals in 1983–84.

4. Steve Thomas leads the league with 11 career overtime goals compared to Gretzky who had just two overtime goals in regular-season play.

5. Dale Hawerchuk recorded a league-best five assists in the second period against Los Angeles on March 6, 1984. Gretzky's best period saw him earn three assists.

6. Darryl Sittler scored an amazing 10 points against Boston on February 7, 1976, a record never equalled even by Gretzky, whose best was two eight-point games.

7. Bryan Trottier's record six-point period on December 23, 1978, leads all NHLers, including Gretzky who had numerous four-point periods.

8. Mike Gartner amassed 17 30-goal seasons; Gretzky had 14.

9. Mike Bossy recorded nine consecutive 50-goal seasons, one better than Gretzky's eight with Edmonton.

10. Harry Broadbent has held the record for the longest consecutive goal-scoring streak since 1921–22 when he scored in 16 straight games, a mark few modern-day players have challenged, including Gretzky who has a personal-high nine-game streak.

Game 5: Bloodlines

Pavel/Valeri Bure
Frank/Pete Mahovlich
Bobby/Brett Hull
Max/Doug Bentley
Phil/Tony Esposito
Gordie/Mark Howe
Kevin/Derian Hatcher
Scott/Rob Niedermayer
Geoff/Russ Courtnall
Maurice/Henri Richard
Dale/Dave Hunter
Brian/Brent Sutter
Eric/Brett Lindros
Pierre/Sylvain Turgeon
Neal/Aaron Broten
Ken/Dave Dryden
Daniel/Henrik Sedin
Wayne/Brent Gretzky
Joe/Brian Mullen
Peter/Anton Stastny
Marcel/Gilbert Dionne
Chris/Sean Pronger

Game 6: Olympic Mettle

1. N. Gold 2002/Canada, Mario Lemieux
2. C. Silver 2002/USA, Brett Hull
3. H. Bronze 2002/Russia, Alexei Yashin
4. I. Gold 1998/Czech Re., Dominik Hasck
5. J. Silver 1998/Russia, Pavel Bure
6. G. Bronze 1998/Finland, Teemu Selanne
7. F. Gold 1994/Sweden, Peter Forsberg
8. A. Silver 1994/Canada, Paul Kariya
9. M. Bronze 1994/Finland, Saku Koivu
10. L. Gold 1992/Unified Team, Nikolai Khabibulin
11. E. Silver 1992/Canada, Eric Lindros
12. K. Bronze 1992/Czech Re., Robert Lang
13. B. Gold 1988/USSR, Alexander Mogilny
14. D. Gold 1984/USSR, Igor Larionov

Game 7: Odd Man Out

1. Steve Yzerman
2. Brett Hull
3. Chris Pronger
4. Mario Lemieux
5. Patrick Roy
6. Dave Schultz
7. Gerry Cheevers
8. Marcel Dionne
9. Wayne Gretzky
10. Phil Esposito

Game 8: MVP Maverick

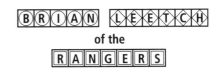

As of 2001, only one non-Canadian has won MVP status in the postseason: Brian Leetch of the New York Rangers in 1994.

ACKNOWLEDGEMENTS

Thanks to the following publishers and organizations for the use of quoted and statistical material:

- *The Hockey News,* various excerpts. Reprinted by permission of *The Hockey News,* a division of GTC Transcontinental Publishing, Inc.
- *The National Post.*
- *Total Hockey.* By Dan Diamond and Associates, Inc. Published by Total Sports, (1998).
- *The Montreal Gazette.*
- *The Globe and Mail.*
- *The Official NHL Guide and Record Book.* Published by Total Sports Canada.
- *When the Final Buzzer Sounds.* Edited by Charles Wilkins, with Colleen and Gordie Howe. Published by Triumph Books (2000).
- *The Rangers.* By Brian McFarlane. Published by Stoddart (1997).

Care has been taken to trace ownership of copyright material contained in this book. The publishers welcome any information that will enable them to rectify any reference or credit in subsequent editions.

The authors gratefully acknowledges the help of Steve Dryden and everyone at *The Hockey News;* Gary Meagher and Benny Ercolani of the NHL; Phil Pritchard at the Hockey Hall of Fame; the staff at the McLellan-Redpath Library at McGill University; Rob Sanders and Chris Labonte at Greystone Books; the many hockey writers, broadcast-journalists, media and Internet organizations who have made the game better through their own work; as well as editor Christine Kondo for her patience, dedication and expertise, Webmaster Mike Curran, graphic artists Peter van Vlaardingen and Peter Cocking and puzzle designer Adrian van Vlaardingen for their creativity.